This is
ourFaith

Copyright © **Redemptorist Publications**
Wolf's Lane, Chawton, Hampshire GU34 3HQ
Telephone 01420 88222 Fax 01420 88805
rp@rpbooks.co.uk   www.rpbooks.co.uk

A registered charity limited by guarantee
Registered in England 3261721

Original text: Rosemary Gallagher, Fr John Trenchard and Jeffrey John
Revised edition 2014

Original design: Orchid Design
Revised edition design: Eliana Thompson

First printed January 1995
Revised November 2001
Second revised edition May 2014
Reprinted February 2019 (13th printing)

ISBN 978-0-85231-408-1

© Photographs:
CorbisStockmarket, Photodisc, Inc., David Toase, APA, John Crone, Grant Pritchard,
Metropolitan Musem of Art, Bequest of Isaac D Fletcher, 1917. Mr and Mrs Isaac D. Fletcher Collection.
Last Supper: Rembrandt. The Supper of Emmaus 1648 (detail), Statens Museum for Kunst, Copenhagen.
Shutterstock.com: BasPhoto; lev radin; 1000 Words; jorisvo; Elena Mirage; Jurand; Gandolfo Camatella.

Redemptorist Publications is indebted, for biblical citations, to the translators and publishers of
the Jerusalem Bible, copyright © 1966 by Darton, Longman & Todd, Ltd and Doubleday,
a division of Random House, Inc. Reprinted by permission.

Printed in Britain by
Orchard Press Cheltenham Ltd

This is
ourFaith

a popular presentation
of Anglican belief

redemptorist
publications

contents

The Spirit of life

From the moment we're born life is full of surprises.

There are good times, bad times, sad times, happy times.

How do we make sense of this experience called life?

What does it mean – this roller coaster of

joy and heartbreak, hope

and disillusion?

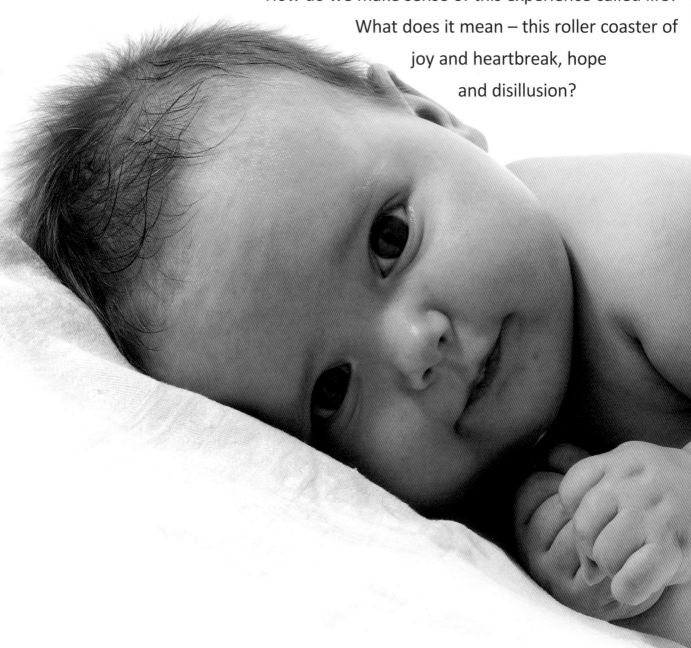

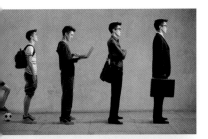

From the moment we're born we begin to try to make sense of life. Our struggles as a baby are signs of conflict between ourselves and the world into which we have been born.

We start life with a strong sense of self-value and self-preservation which strengthens and directs our actions and our inaction. The way in which we develop, and the kind of adults we become, are determined by the way in which this instinctive self-value interacts with the circumstances and relationships we encounter.

By the time we have reached adulthood we like to think we've grown up. We've usually survived a number of painful experiences, we've made mistakes, but we've also had some good experiences. We've grown up.

But that's not the end of the story; it's only the beginning.

All through our life we will continue to ask, "What's it all about?" "What makes sense?" "What doesn't make sense?" Often it is only when we face new experiences that we are conscious that there is something more to life than we have grasped so far.

Happy experiences surprise us with unexpected pleasure, excitement or amazement. Sad and tragic moments leave us feeling confused, lost and asking, "There must be more to life than this?"

"Your whole life is changed once you have a child. I have to think about what I'm doing, where I'm going, how it will affect her. I have to plan my life now. I can no longer just drift aimlessly through my life because I have Sophie to think about and to care for."

"That magic moment of transition"

I remember walking along one day when I was about fifteen. I was at that stage in life when you yo-yo between feeling grown-up and yet feeling still very much part of school life. It was a hot, muggy day. A day that makes you feel summer will never end and being at school will never end. Teachers, exams, parents not understanding you: that seemed to be the total horizon of my life. Suddenly, a small toddler ran out in front of me. The child was laughing excitedly as his older sister chased him. Lost in the merriment, he crashed straight into me as his mother shouted, "Mind that man!"

Her words hit me ten times harder than her son. I saw myself in a new light. The monotony of the endlessness of that hot summer day dissolved into a new image of myself as a man. I was no longer a child, somebody's son, a schoolboy. I was a man. A stranger had recognised that, had said so. It was a fleeting moment yet now, years later, I recall it as a turning point.

Recently, a similar incident happened again and as I heard those words, "Mind that man", all the original feelings flooded back and I relived that magic moment of transition from boy to man.

"I've been pulled out of myself"

Giving birth to my little girl, Sophie, seemed to bring everything in my life into perspective. I sometimes think now that I wish I had extra time. And then I look back, before Sophie, when I had all the time in the world and I wonder what I did with it. I don't know. I didn't even seem to notice it.

I get so much out of having her. Your whole life is changed once you have a child. I have to think about what I'm doing, where I'm going, how it will affect her. I have to plan my life now. I can no longer just drift aimlessly through, because I have Sophie to think about and to care for. I have been pulled out of myself and forced to think beyond my own world. It's an amazing experience. As I say, everything seems to be more in perspective since I've had her.

"I've worked out what matters to me"

When my partner left me for someone else I was shattered. I didn't think our relationship was perfect but we had been through a number of ups and downs, survived and, I thought, grown closer as a result. I couldn't believe that this was the end. Yet I wasn't sure whether I could rebuild something that had been so deliberately smashed by someone I had trusted.

I felt rejected, humiliated and, later, angry, very angry. It was the usual story: everyone else seemed to know about the affair before me. Our children were confused, they asked questions I couldn't answer, they needed support, reassurance and patient handling. The problem was I needed these things too so it was difficult for all of us. We limped along for many months.

The only news we heard from their father seemed to be that he had made the right decision. Bully for him! It didn't help us at all.

Eventually, I started to pick up the pieces. I began to look at myself, my life, the children's future, and who and what we had become. I was forced to reassess almost every part of my existence and, looking back, it was a good exercise. Before he left, we were chugging along in a happy cocoon. Life ran through my fingers like dry sand from the beach. Now I value everything so much more, I've worked out what matters to me.

"A restlessness had stirred in me"

I don't know what caused my breakdown really. It wasn't a single event or crisis. In fact, I was walking through the park on my way to work last spring, when a feeling of utter desolation swept over me. I was surrounded by signs of new life: bulbs in flower, the birds chattering and my heart felt like lead.

I have a successful career, enough money, a pleasant home, and a wife and family who give me security and a sense of belonging. And yet my life seems strangely empty and meaningless.

The feeling of isolation and being adrift on a sea of nothingness is powerful and all-pervading. Throughout last summer those feelings of dissatisfaction and almost a desperate kind of loneliness seeped into my days. My wife showed kindly concern and put it down to the midlife crisis. She assured me it would pass.

But a restlessness had stirred in me. Material possessions and human achievement are somehow not enough anymore. I have begun to read more and listen to other people as they talk about their philosophy or way of life. I am conscious of searching for something to complete my incompleteness. I know there must be more meaning to life than what I have experienced. I think recognising that is an important step for me.

"I love you"

The words are commonplace yet, to me, they meant very little. I wanted sex (who doesn't?) but I also wanted non-involvement and my independence. These are the strengths that I was taught even as a child. As it became clearer that she loved me I remember that my reaction was to run away. I told her not to nag me and to leave me alone. Then, when she did leave me alone (she was used to dealing with children), I reacted angrily.

One cold winter evening, I was lost more than usual in frustration and tears. I remember saying, "If I tell you I love you, that means more than I can give you." I wanted to escape but she held me in her arms. It must have been her warmth that took me out of myself to say, "I love you."

"I didn't think I would be able to get through it"

Lots of people in my school come from divorced families but I didn't know it at the time my parents split up. They used to row a lot and I was very afraid that they would separate. I didn't think I would be able to get through it but now I've experienced it I know you can if you persevere.

When my Dad walked out, I was worried that my Mum would leave as well. I thought it was my fault that he went in the end. My sister and I had a row and he was cross. I thought I wouldn't see him again.

We didn't know what was happening for about two days. He just went and my Mum didn't say anything; then she told us. I felt all churned up inside as though no one cared what was happening to me and my sister. I kept hoping he would come back, that things would be the same as before and we would be a proper family. I got so that I didn't want to talk to anyone. I used to fight with my sister and break her things. I felt cut off, I thought everyone else had a Dad except me.

Now my Dad has got a new wife and we see him about three or four times a year. I've got used to it now. We've moved three times and that's hard; new friends, new school, new home.

Some friends are helpful, others are not: they just spread what you tell them around the school. If you don't have anyone to talk to, you just have to try to trust someone. I get very sad sometimes when I've seen my Dad and we have to go home. I don't know if I want to get married because I think the same thing is going to happen to me and it frightens me.

"I feel I've given him his life back"

When my second son, Alan, was born, the doctors at the hospital told me that he was suffering from a dysplastic kidney condition that prevented his kidney growing. We waited for over two years for a donor but without success. I couldn't face the thought of the little chap growing up year after year with uncertainty and dialysis treatment every day. I decided to ask the doctors if I would be a suitable donor. Alan and I had our operations on the same day and the whole thing has been a great success. I feel I've given him his life back.

Life's difficult but it's still worth living. At least now Alan's got a chance. I'm only an ordinary working man but I feel overwhelmed that I could give my child such a gift. I don't really know what to make of it.

"Lord, you have made us for yourself alone, and our hearts will always be restless until they find their rest in you."

Saint Augustine

Change never leaves us as it finds us

As we journey through life we face continual change and from time to time sudden change which stops us in our tracks. Our personal map for living life, which we had worked out so well, is somehow no longer applicable. It doesn't fit our new and changed experience and we have to redraw it, once again.

At the heart of all this tension, change and complexity of life remain those fundamental questions, "What is life all about, where am I going, what does it all mean?" And the root of these questions takes us back to our first days of life when we were at the centre of our tiny world; a time before we had been forced to adapt and adjust to the world and the people around us. That sense of total self-worth, self-value, is the most important treasure we possess. And in the changes, the kind of changes that we have looked at which people experience, we can learn to extend ourselves into an even more complete wholeness of being, unique, precious and of irreplaceable value. This is a wholeness built not on isolation or power, but on the completion of the potential we had as a newly born person.

It is a paradox that we can only reach that full potential of ourselves through our interaction with others and through a willingness for and an acceptance of change as part of life. Facing change can always help us to grow.

Yet we fear change; we are afraid of things never being the same, afraid of the unknown, afraid that change will demolish us. And so we avoid change as much as possible. We tend to refuse to face new changes in our lives and in our bodies because we want to cling to what is familiar, what is known. In one sense we are like an unborn child still within the womb. Such a child is safe, warm, protected from the outside world. But such a child is also growing, developing, maturing. There comes a time when the womb can no longer contain the child or supply all that is needed for continued growth and development. Birth is imminent: a major life change, from all that is familiar, safe, tried and tested into unknown territory with only our potential to bring with us.

Each of us has been through that major life change of birth into a totally new world. And every change we have negotiated since will have been a mini-birth in terms of new experience and growth. Only when we have resisted or refused change have we stopped growing, stopped learning and begun to kill off our potential for life.

What is this life force then which pulls us on, often in spite of our resistance and reluctance? Why do we experience a restlessness and dissatisfaction with life even when we have ample material goods? Where does that powerful magnet we call love come from? The kind of love that makes us feel brand new again, whole, full of life and enthusiasm?

The starting point of our Christian faith is our own human experience. If you look back on your own life, you will recall experiences that were successful and happy but also remember experiences that were painful and which stretched you to the limit. Looking back on such experiences forces us to look forward and to recognise that there seems no limit to the human spirit. This is equally true of the life of the human race.

It is our Christian faith that every single person is touched by God and that the experiences that draw us to a deeper sense of our self-value and the greatness of the human spirit are the work of God within us.

The experience of many people throughout the ages has led them to believe that there is something more to life than simply what they see and understand from their senses. For a large number, the answer has been a belief system or a religion. But many people will say that religion doesn't provide the answers. In fact, in their search for meaning in life, they often reject religion as hypocritical, a power structure or a myth which pacifies and tranquillises those who cannot face the fundamental truths of life.

Such a reaction is a wholly sound one on which to base any search for the meaning of life because it is founded upon a search for truth and authenticity. It is the search for something which makes sense of human experience and which will not be fobbed off only by second-hand answers dealt out by others, rather than answers which ring true to a personal experience of life.

In his book *The Road Less Travelled,* Dr Scott Peck poses the question which must be at the heart of any serious attempt to understand the meaning of life and the meaning of a religious response to our questioning. He asks whether the question is really, "What has God done to humans?" or should it rather be, "What have humans done to God?"

All too often human beings, in talking about God or explaining the meaning of their religion, teach us more about human nature than about the nature of God. When we look at the history of people's religious quest we see it overlaid with human characteristics which have often distorted or muddied any images or experiences of God.

And yet the rumour of the Spirit of God remains as strong as ever in the hearts and lives of men and women. Even those who claim to have no belief in God will often admit to praying in times of serious need or loss.

The spiritual dimension within each one of us is a call to something beyond ourselves. It is a hunger of the heart: a longing for something more, a relationship which will complete us and fulfil our unspoken need. True religion is not the imposition of sets of rules: it is the discovery of a relationship which helps us make sense of life and leads us to the fullness of life.

Throughout history men and women have tried hard to find meaning in their existence and their experiences. We have always asked the questions: What is the meaning and purpose of life? What is upright behaviour and what is sinful? Where does suffering originate and why do we suffer? How can genuine happiness be found? What happens at death? What is the ultimate mystery from which we take our origin and towards which we tend?

The rumour of the

Islam, Christianity and **Judaism** are known as "Abrahamic" faiths, because they all trace their roots back to Abraham. The name "Islam" means "submission (to God)", and that is the path Muslims are called to follow. They worship God, who is one, almighty and merciful. They strive to submit to God's plan and, in this, follow Abraham. They do not, however, acknowledge Jesus Christ as God although they venerate him as a prophet and honour Mary, his virgin mother. They follow the teaching of the *Qu'ran*, given to the prophet Muhammad (who lived about AD 600) who, they believe, gives them the final revelation of the true path to God.

Buddhism is a very long-established religious tradition which dates back to the sixth century BC. It is a way of life which centres on the teaching of the Buddha who leads a path to enlightenment based on the *four Noble Truths* – the fact of pain or evil; that pain has a cause; that pain can be ended; and that it can be ended by following the *Eightfold Way* – of right views, right intention, right speech, right action, right livelihood, right effort, right mindfulness and right concentration. This enlightenment is said to testify to the essential inadequacy of this changing world, and to the possibility of reaching supreme illumination.

Hinduism is really a comprehensive group of many beliefs and practices, all of which centre on the worship of different gods and on guidance by *gurus*. Hinduism varies enormously from place to place and there is a wide range of structures, festivals and caste systems associated with it. As with Buddhism, the ultimate goal is deliverance from the cycle of continual birth and death, and release is sought from the trials of the present life by ascetic practices, profound meditation and recourse to God in confidence and love.

As Christians we respect the many rich insights, manner of life and teachings of other religions, recognising their significant contribution to the search for truth. The Christian Church, however, has a particular closeness to the religion known as Judaism.

Judaism provides the foundation of faith for followers of Jesus Christ. Jesus was a Jew and we can only fully understand him in the light of his Jewish heritage. The beginnings of Christian belief are to be found in the faith and election – by the one true God – of Abraham, the patriarchs, Moses and the prophets. This revelation of himself by God, which called into being the Jewish people, is recorded in the books known to the Jews as the *Torah,* together with other texts, and to Christians as the *Old Testament*.

The developments in the universal search for meaning can be seen in the diversity of world religions

Spirit of God

פָּקַד בְּמֵי מְרִיבַת מַיִם , צְמֵאִים
זֻגּוּ : תַּעֲנֶה קְדוֹשִׁים מְנַסְּכִים לְךָ מַיִם
שְׁתוֹת מַיִם חֲלִילָה פֶּן וְנֶסֶךְ לְךָ מַיִם , וְהַצְלִיחָה נָא וְהוֹשִׁיעָה נָא : לְמַעַן רֹאשׁ מִי
תַּעֲנֶה שׁוֹאֲלִים בִּרְבּוּעַ אֶשְׁלֵי מַיִם , וְהוֹשִׁיעָה נָא : לְמַעַן תֵּל
מַיִם , תִּפְתַּח אֶרֶץ וְהַרְעִיף שָׁמַיִם , וְהַצְלִיחָה נָא וְהוֹשִׁיעֵנוּ אֵל
נָא קְהַל עֲדַת יְשֻׁרוּן . סֶלָה וּמְחַל עֲ.

The Old Testament

Our human experience and our search for meaning is recorded in a unique way in what Christians call the "Old Testament". It is unique for two reasons:

■ Firstly, it records the struggle of a people – the Jewish people – to make sense of life and, in particular, to enter into a relationship with God.

■ Secondly, and much more importantly, it records the struggle of God to enter into a relationship with his chosen people.

Let's look at both these statements:

Firstly, the Jewish people were unique in their growing realisation that there is only one God. Other peoples worshipped the gods of nature or the gods of their ancestors. In the thousand years prior to the birth of Jesus Christ the Jews came to recognise that there is only one God, the creator of the universe, who was intimately involved in their happiness and success. This was not an easy process. There were times in Jewish history when they were exiled from their own country, and suffered the most dreadful agonies and humiliations yet, as time went on, they grew in their understanding of God's love.

Secondly (and, again, much more importantly), God is recognised in the Old Testament as taking the initiative in letting himself be known to his people. And God is not seen in the Old Testament as remote or uncaring but, rather, as "moved by compassion" to care for his people. So startling is this "revelation" – a truth that could never be conceived of by human effort – that the Old Testament is described as the "word of God".

Perhaps one of the closest human parallels to the relationship between God and the Jewish people is the love between parent and child. It is a relationship of total dependency but not without its difficult moments and tensions. There are frustrations on both sides as they struggle towards mutual understanding and intimacy. In the Jewish people of the Old Testament we see the effort to be "grown-up", to "make a name for themselves" – to be like God; and in the God of the Old Testament we see the frustration of every parent to make their love known to their child – it is the Lord who "will wipe away the tears from every cheek" and who is "like someone who lifts an infant close against his cheek, stooping down to him to give him his food".

For most people today the Old Testament is not an "easy read". This is not because its message lacks excitement or because the stories lack lustre. On the contrary! Yet some guidance is helpful in reading the Old Testament, which comes to us not as a single book beginning on page 1 and continuing for many pages, but as a collection of over thirty-nine books and writings assembled over the period of nearly a thousand years. It is a "library", much of which we should dip into rather than attempt to read at a single sitting. For the follower of Jesus Christ, the Old Testament is essential reading. It is necessary for the following reasons:

■ The Old Testament reveals a wholly unique relationship between the one God and a specially chosen people. The God who is revealed and worshipped by the Jews is the one whom Jesus was to call his "Father".

■ The Old Testament asks questions and tackles the issues that confront every human being. The Jews faced the most difficult questions. The answers to those questions were the result of much searching and only finally realised in the life and work of Jesus Christ.

■ The world of the Old Testament was the world into which Jesus Christ was born. Even as a young boy of three he would be taught the essentials of the story of his people. As he started school he was probably given a slate with passages of scripture (the Old Testament) written on it. The slate would have been smeared with honey – a sign of the teaching he was to absorb. In his sufferings Jesus reflected the life of the Jewish people of the Old Testament. Many of his teachings were taken directly from the Old Testament.

The Old Testament, then, "foreshadows" the life of Jesus Christ. It gives an outline or shape of what is to come in Jesus Christ. The Old Testament provides us with an outline picture of God. And Jesus Christ throws light on this picture so that the face of God is fully revealed. As St Augustine of Hippo was to write: "In the Old Testament the New is hidden; in the New Testament the Old is laid open."

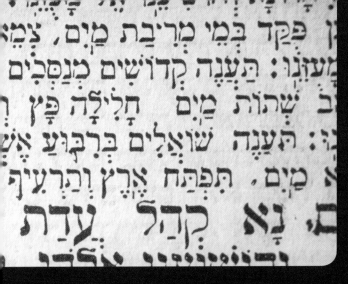

The principle names of God's chosen people used in the Old Testament:

Hebrew This originally meant "nomad", literally, "one from across the river" (a reference to the exodus of God's people from Egypt). It is the name usually given to the Jews of earlier times and also to the language.

Jew This is derived from "Judah", one of the sons of Jacob. The tribe gave its name to the kingdom of Judah and became the nucleus of the Jewish people.

Israel This is the name given to the Jewish people. It was given to Jacob as ancestor of the people by God: "You shall no longer be called Jacob, but Israel"(Genesis 32:28). "Israel" means "God struggles" or "God is strong".

The most important texts of the Old Testament

The most important texts of the Old Testament are its first five books which make up the Torah or Pentateuch. The Pentateuch outlines:

■ How God "chose" Israel to be his own people, beginning with his promise to Abraham to make him the "father of a multitude of nations... and his descendants as many as the stars of heaven" (Genesis 17:5; 22:17).

■ How God made a "covenant" or "contract" with the Jews to make them the channel of his mercy if they kept the laws he gave them. And so to Moses, the dominant figure of the Pentateuch and the whole Old Testament, God says, "I will take you as my people, and I will be your God" (Exodus 6:7).

■ How God gave the Law to Israel as the most direct revelation of his will. This is symbolised in the tradition that the Ten Commandments were originally inscribed by God on two tablets of stone. The Lord said, "I am the Lord your God, who rescued you from Egypt where you were slaves.

1. "Worship no god but me. Do not make for yourselves images of anything in heaven or on earth or in the water under the earth. Do not bow down to any idol or worship it, for I am the Lord your God and I tolerate no rivals.
2. Do not use my name for evil purposes, for I, the Lord your God will punish anyone who misuses my name.
3. Observe the sabbath and keep it holy, as I, the Lord your God have commanded you.
4. Respect your father and your mother.
5. Do not commit murder.
6. Do not commit adultery.
7. Do not steal.
8. Do not accuse anyone falsely.
9. Do not desire another man's wife.
10. Do not desire his house, his land, his slaves, his cattle, his donkeys or anything else he owns" (Deuteronomy 5:6-21).

The names of God

There are two principal names for God in the Old Testament.

Yahweh: This name is probably from the verb "to be", meaning "to be present and active". It is the name revealed to Moses. It is considered so holy that it is never said aloud. Instead, it is replaced by "Elohim".

Elohim: This name is from the plural of "God" and means "one who possesses all the divine attributes".

which translated means:

God [Elohim] said to Moses, "I Am who I Am [Yahweh]" Exodus 3:14.

The moment when God revealed his name to Moses comes in one of the most significant passages in the Bible: "Moses said to God, 'If I come to the Israelites and say to them, "The God of your ancestors has sent me to you", and they ask me, "What is his name?" what shall I say to them?' God said to Moses, 'I Am who I Am.' He said further, 'Thus you shall say to the Israelites, "I Am has sent me to you."' God also said to Moses, 'Thus you shall say to the Israelites, "The Lord, the God of your ancestors, the God of Abraham, the God of Isaac, and the God of Jacob, has sent me to you." This is my name for ever, and this my title for all generations'" (Exodus 3:13-15).

Is the Old

Jesus Christ did not burst in on a world wholly unprepared for him. Looking back we can recognise in the Old Testament how God was preparing a way for the coming of Jesus Christ.

If we look back to the Old Testament and try to pinpoint the single most important event in the history of the Jewish people we would have to say that everything surrounding the "Exodus" from slavery in Egypt was such an event. However, to isolate this moment in such a way would be misleading. It was more their prayerful reflection and deepening understanding of the *meaning* of this event than the event *itself* that formed the Jewish people in their special relationship with God.

It is important, then, to understand what kind of history the Old Testament is. Usually, the Old Testament is divided into three kinds of books – history, poetry (or wisdom) and prophecy. But all the writings – even the history – are concerned with the relationship between the Jews and God. History is not written in the clinical fashion of the modern historian. When, for example, Bishop James Ussher in 1654 used the "information" in the Bible to calculate the creation of the world at 4004 BC he was totally misunderstanding the Old Testament. The Bible has only one purpose and one alone: it tells of the deepening relationship between God and men and women – the single most significant fact of history since creation itself. The Bible is a history of "salvation".

Understanding the meaning of the writing

We believe that "all scripture is inspired by God and can profitably be used for teaching, for refuting error, for guiding people's lives and teaching them to be Holy" (2 Timothy 3:16). But to speak of scripture as "inspired" or as "The word of God" doesn't mean God simply moved the writers' hands like robots! Each book also reflects the background and understanding of its author. Even when provided with a good translation (and no translation can ever be quite like the original), we still have the task of unravelling the meaning of what has been written.

It is obvious that unless we understand the kind of writing that appears in the Old Testament we can make some very silly mistakes. We can totally misread the word of God, just as our second-century-BC Jew could completely fail to grasp what our society is like today through misreading the daily newspapers.

The Old Testament is not history or geography – it's about salvation

There is one, vital fact about the Old Testament which we must always have at the front of our minds. The word of God is concerned with salvation. It is not primarily concerned with history or geography or any form of science. It is concerned with our salvation. It draws to our attention the relationship which exists between God and men and women. And to understand what God is saying about our salvation, we have to pay serious attention to the customary way in which people of the time thought and expressed themselves. We must also bear in mind the customs of the day and the way in which people related to one another and dealt with one another in their day-to-day existence at the time of writing.

The books of the Old Testament

The Old Testament records the struggle of the Jewish people to make sense of life and to enter into a relationship with God. It also records God's relationship with his world and his people.

In conveying this development and growth in understanding of this unique relationship, the Old Testament has been called a library of books and the three main sections of this library are as follows:

History and Law

These books record both the historical story of the Jewish people and also the story of the gift of the Covenant or Law which God gave them. The story of the ways in which they kept or failed to keep the Law is threaded through their years of recorded history.

■ The early years: Genesis, Exodus, Leviticus, Numbers, Deuteronomy.

■ Their settlement and exile: Joshua, Judges, Ruth, 1 and 2 Samuel, 1 and 2 Kings, 1 and 2 Chronicles.

■ Returning from exile to resettlement: Ezra, Nehemiah, Esther.

Wisdom

These books record the customs, worship and understanding of the great thinkers of the Jewish people. In these books we can discover their philosophy of life, their poetry and their understanding of their special relationship with God: Job, Psalms, Proverbs, Ecclesiastes, Song of Solomon.

Prophets

Whilst containing a considerable amount of historical information, these books are principally focused upon the teachings and preaching of the prophets, the wise men of the Jewish people through the ages: Isaiah, Jeremiah, Lamentations, Baruch, Ezekiel, Daniel, Hosea, Joel, Amos, Obadiah, Jonah, Micah, Nahum, Habakkuk, Zephaniah, Haggai, Zechariah, Malachi.

Testament History?

How do Christians deepen their understanding of the Old Testament?

The Old Testament tells the story of the one true God who originally revealed himself over many centuries to a particular people. It starts with the story of how God created the world in the beginning and it follows the story to a time just before the birth of Jesus Christ. During this period the Old Testament was mostly written in Hebrew – the language of the Jewish people. In this way, the word of God was expressed at a particular time in history and in human words.

At the time of Jesus Christ, Jewish boys were probably taught to read Hebrew aloud. However, the everyday spoken languages were Aramaic and Greek. So the Hebrew was translated accordingly. Since then, and helped by the spread of the Christian Church, the Old Testament in its entirety has been translated into numerous languages.

If we are to deepen our understanding of God's word, then, we must understand exactly *what* was written, we must understand *when* it was written, and we must understand *why* it was written.

And so to understand what God is saying to us today through the Old Testament we have to answer two questions:

- What does the text actually say?
- What did it mean to the Jewish people at the time?

Read the six pieces of text on the right and below carefully. The Hebrew piece may prove a little difficult but have a go!

The English pieces are easier. They are all taken from newspapers published on the same day. The piece from the BBC 2 listings won't mean much to you unless you saw the film, nor will the reference to the bar code at Morriston Hospital unless you are a regular supermarket shopper. The book review is clear enough if you are familiar with the workings of the CIA. When we learn that the clip about the husband being persuaded to jump off his broomstick is from a gossip column, we will probably take it with a pinch of salt! The meaning of the horoscope depends on your view of such things.

We can well imagine the confusion in the mind of a native of Palestine about 100 BC – which is when the Hebrew piece was written – if he was faced with these newspaper extracts. Even if provided with a good translation – and how do you translate words like "bar code" and "computerised"? – the meaning of the texts is not self-evident. What is a "brain drain"? Do the inhabitants of this country really direct their lives according to the stars?

Aquarius Week ahead 01902
Jan 21-Feb 19 b8932

The sun is in Scorpio now brings matters of a career or professional nature into sharp focus and somewhere along the line you must be prepared to go against the tide of opinion and do what you should have done six months ago.

March 2001

non-fiction
JOSEPH LOSEY

The account of the life of film director Joseph Losey represents the other side of the CIA coin, for Losey was forced into exile after the House of the Un-American Activities Committee labelled him a communist.

In so doing the Americans lost one of their cinema greats: Losey, after a brief and troubled career in Hollywood, went on to become one of the most famous directors in the French and British film industry.

I would gladly pay their airfare myself and, in extreme cases, be quite happy to rustle up unmarried female relatives of my American husband who might be persuaded to jump the broomstick if a Green Card were in the balance.

Whatever, just go will you? Remember the Brain Drain, in the seventies? - we could call this the Pain Drain. As in Pain in the **** - but no this is a family newspaper.

TRAIN FO

Informatio
program
today's
additiona
may be r
certain p
Call Tod

BBC 2

6.00pm Director/Designer William Cameron Menzies '50s fantasy favourite about a small-town American kid (Jimmy Hunt) who sees a flying saucer land but nobody believes him. It explores the paranoid 1950s territory of *Alien* possession, best exemplified by Don Siegel's 1956 masterpiece *Invasion of the Body Snatchers*.

In a pioneering scheme at Morriston Hospital, patients are being issued with their own unique bar code, rather like a can of baked beans in a supermarket. But the only trolley they are likely to come near is the one used on the drug rounds.

The bar code is strapped to the patients wrist and acts as a form of identification. So on ward rounds when the ward sister scans the code, like a shop assistant, details of the patient's prescription flashes up on the screen of a computerised drugs cabinet. The patient's bar code is cross referenced with the one input by the Doctor at the time of prescribing, and the one on the bottle of drugs in the cabinet.

וֹן פָּקַד בְּמֵי מְרִיבַת מָיִם, צִמְאִים לְהַשְׁקוֹתָם מַיִם. וְהַצְלִיחָה נָא

שַׁעֲנוּ: תַּעֲנֶה קְדוֹשִׁים מְנַסְּבִים לְךָ מַיִם, וְהוֹשִׁיעָה נָא: לְמַעַן רֹאשׁ

שָׁרוֹת מַיִם הָלִילָה פֶּן וְנָסַל לְךָ מַיִם, וְהַצְלִיחָה נָא וְחֹ

The Psalms

The psalms are prayers of people who regarded God as a friend. There was no need to hide their true feelings when they were in God's presence. And so when they prayed, they complained, they questioned, they cajoled. At first sight, some of the things they said to God surprise us. We have a way when we pray of wanting to keep a stiff upper lip and be on our best behaviour. This was not the approach taken by the psalmists. If things were bad then there was no point in glossing over the badness in order to impress God. There was no misfortune or misery which God would not understand.

So they meant what they said when they talked about being wronged, hurt, even rejected. God was not above and beyond all this. It was his world and he held the reins. The famous Psalm 22 prayed by Jesus on the cross is a good illustration of this:

My God, my God, why have you forsaken me?
You are far from my plea and the cry of my distress.
O my God, I call by day and you give no reply;
I call by night and I find no peace (Psalm 22:1-2).

If the prayer had ended there or simply continued in that vein, then it might have been open to the criticism that it was indulging in self-pity or bitterness. But it did not end there. After they had said how badly they felt, they were able to step outside of themselves and look to God. Invariably there followed a protestation of confidence in the Almighty. Contrary to appearances, he had not left them. He could never abandon them. His help was sure to come. Nothing was more certain than that.

Yet you, O God, are holy,
enthroned on the praises of Israel.
In you our fathers put their trust;
they trusted and you set them free.
When they cried to you, they escaped.
In you they trusted and never in vain (Psalm 22:3-5).

With this renewed trust in God they went on to make their petitions. This they did in a restrained way. Their requests were made in general terms. There was no need to suggest to God what he might do. They were sure that he would do something and they could safely leave to his wisdom the choice of what was to be done.

It is interesting to see that, in these psalms, a process is going on which soothes the human spirit. People who start off their prayer with their spirits at a low ebb work through to a trust in God which results in a restrained but confident plea for God's continuing protection.

O Lord, do not leave me alone, my strength,
make haste to help me!
Rescue my soul from the sword
(Psalm 22:19-20).

The Spirit of the Lord has been given to me

A Messiah on the horizon

The Old Testament records God's relationship with his people and the ways in which he communicated his message to them through their experiences and through their prophets. At the heart of this relationship was the promise and the growing confidence that a Messiah would come. God would send his people a new leader, a king, a guide to freedom, peace and fulfilment. A Messiah was on the horizon for the people of God.

The Christ, the Messiah and the Jews

The people of Nazareth would have been amazed to know that some people nowadays think that "Christ" is the surname of Jesus. For them the Christ, whom they called in their own language the Messiah, was the hope of Israel. He would come and restore the glory which their greatest king, David, had brought to Israel. Not only would he restore their lost glory but he would make them the greatest nation on earth.

The great questions in the synagogues were about the Christ. When would he come? What would he be like?

In Jesus' time, and particularly when he lived in Galilee, there was a great deal of disagreement about the answer to these questions. One Galilean group called the Zealots believed that the coming of Christ was imminent and, to prepare the country for his coming, they resorted to guerrilla tactics to overthrow the foreign government of Rome. Another group, the Essenes, who lived in a sort of community at Qumran, near the Dead Sea, believed that two Christs would come: one would be their priest, the other would be their king.

All the Jews believed that it was essential to prepare for the coming of the Christ. They didn't necessarily agree, however, on how they should prepare. A group called the Pharisees followed a very strict way of life which kept them apart from all foreigners. They felt it was necessary for the Jews to be a "people apart" for only then would they understand the message the Christ would preach.

Although the Jews had different ideas about the sort of person the Christ would be, they eagerly looked forward to his coming. The followers of Jesus had grown up against this background of expectancy. They, like everyone else, looked forward to the coming of the Christ.

In the event many rejected Jesus because he didn't fit in with any of their ideas of what Christ should be.

Looking back, it's easy for us to see that the coming of Jesus Christ was indeed a turning point in the history of men and women. A new era did begin in Nazareth all those years ago. But it was not the era expected by the reformers, the Zealots, the establishment or the scholars of the time. It was something that perhaps most people had never dared hope for, this era of the kingdom of God, a God whose whole being was a commitment to love. This means that God is in control of his world and everything will be safe and in good hands – all will be well. Suffering, pain or rejection will be overcome in death if not in life because our earthly death is not the end of life; for those who choose to accept God's promise, it is the beginning of eternal life. All will be well because our God is a God of infinite love, the kind of love we could indeed only dream of in this world before the coming of Jesus of Nazareth.

That is the Good News that Jesus preached: that the kingdom of God had arrived, the promise of God was given already, no one had to wait for death. It arrived in the heart of each person who believed and accepted this love of God. It arrived when each person accepted the gift of God's love in spite of their human situation, their ignorance or their selfishness. It arrives when we start to trust in that love, that promise of God.

As we know from our own experiences it's often only after an event, when we look back on it, that we can see its true significance and its effect upon us. Only on reflection do we understand what has happened to us. It was the same with men and women's experience and understanding of Jesus Christ. They listened to him, they saw miraculous signs, but only gradually, as the years went by, did they really begin to grasp the full significance of his words, his actions and his life.

The final prophet: John

The last prophet in the history of God's relationship with men and women pointed to the presence of the Lord, the Messiah in their midst. John the Baptist was a Jew; he had no fixed home but moved around Judaea and the banks of the River Jordan calling on people to change their ways, to claim their true freedom by training themselves in virtue and turning back wholeheartedly to God. He baptised people in the river water as a sign of their change of heart and their readiness to be open to the Spirit of God speaking in their hearts.

People believed that John the Baptist was the man that the prophet Isaiah spoke of when he wrote hundreds of years earlier:

> "A voice cries in the wilderness:
> Prepare a way for the Lord,
> make his paths straight" (Isaiah 40:3).

> "A feeling of expectancy had grown among the people" (Luke 3:15).

John was known to be a very good, very sincere man. Even Jewish historians of the time recorded this fact. It was not surprising, then, that many people began to think that John was the much longed-for Messiah. For an oppressed people, as the Jews were at that time, a new king bringing freedom and liberation seemed the answer to their prayers.

But John was quick to point out to his many followers that he was simply the forerunner, the link between the laws of the Old Testament and the new era, whereby the gift of the Spirit of God, given in baptism, would characterise a new dimension of God's relationship with his people. Men and women were to be born again in God's Spirit in order to become fully united with their creator, the source of all real love.

John baptises Jesus

One day, when John was baptising people in the River Jordan, a man called Jesus of Nazareth appeared through the crowd and asked for baptism. John's reaction is significant: he tries to dissuade Jesus, claiming that it is Jesus who should baptise him. But Jesus insists, and Jesus' baptism by John becomes the sign that the preparation for the coming of the Messiah is over. Jesus of Nazareth is the Messiah; the Spirit of God is seen to be with him, and the new age which will fulfil and perfect the old one has thereby begun.

"After his baptism, Jesus came to Nazareth, where he had been brought up, and went into the synagogue on the sabbath day as he usually did. He stood up to read and they handed him the scroll of the prophet Isaiah. Unrolling the scroll he found the place where it is written:

> **The spirit of the Lord has been given to me,**
> **for he has anointed me. He has sent me to bring the good**
> **   news to the poor,**
> **to proclaim liberty to captives**
> **and to the blind new sight,**
> **to set the downtrodden free,**
> **to proclaim the Lord's year of favour.**

He then rolled up the scroll, gave it back to the assistant and sat down. And all eyes in the synagogue were fixed on him. Then he began to speak to them, 'This text is being fulfilled today even as you listen'" (Luke 4:18-21).

These words were the starting point of the life work of Jesus. And immediately they presented a challenge to those who heard him. Some were "astonished by the gracious words that came from his lips". Others doubted his credentials and tried to kill him. This is a recurring pattern of reaction throughout the life of Jesus. There is constant tension between those who can accept his words and those who find them intolerable.

Who is Jesus Christ?

Four days dead

Yesterday in the little village of Bethany two miles from Jerusalem, a man was brought back to life after lying in the grave for four days.

Witnesses at the scene claim they saw the rabbi Jesus approach the grave and order the stone to be removed...

Two thousand years ago there were no newspapers and so the above report could only have been spread by word of mouth. Nonetheless, we might expect that if the marvellous words and deeds recorded in the Gospels are genuine, the exciting news they contain would have exploded throughout the known world.

And yet the truth is that Jesus Christ is barely mentioned outside the Gospels. Critics of our faith are quick to seize on this: "If Jesus did all that you claim," they object, "why was his life so little known and why did it end in such humiliation? Surely, an impartial observer must have written something about this extraordinary man?"

How, then, did Jesus appear to those who lived with him? For a moment, let us travel back in time and ask one of them, "Who is Jesus?" We might get the following information.

Jesus grew up in a town called Nazareth in the northern province of Galilee. The little town was a very busy place in Jesus' time as it lies near the great crossroads of the caravan trade routes. Here, as he grew up, Jesus would have met and spoken to merchants and traders from all over the known world.

The people in Jerusalem, 90 miles to the south, didn't have much time for the Galileans. They thought that they mixed rather too much with foreigners and spoke with a rough, vulgar accent.

Galilee was the sort of place you made jokes about and Galileans were the sort of people you jeered. So when Nathanael, a man who later became one of Jesus' followers, first heard about Jesus, he laughingly asked, "Can anything good come out of Nazareth?"

Jesus probably began his life as a village carpenter. At first he seemed to do quite well for himself. He became a rabbi – a teacher of the scriptures. Gradually, his reputation spread, and he began to be accepted as a man who was successfully trying to get to the heart of the Jewish faith.

But then he went too far. Priests and people knew that reforms were needed, but when the religious authorities realised that this man was demanding more than the alteration of a few laws, they got impatient. They persuaded the Roman Governor that it would be in his best interests to have Jesus executed, which he did.

Those are the facts. Not much to write about, is there? Unless, of course, the writer believed that Jesus really was God. The writers who did believe this wrote down his life in the Gospels.

It should be clear that if we went back to ask someone who knew him, "Who is Jesus?", the reply would have been more than a few facts. We would probably get one of the following statements:

1 "They hanged Jesus of Nazareth on the eve of the Passover because he practised sorcery and was leading Israel astray."

2 "You can all be certain that God has made this Jesus whom you crucified both Lord and Christ."

Which of these statements do you agree with? The first is by a Jewish historian who lived at the same time as Christ, the second is by St Peter on the day of Pentecost. You obviously cannot agree with both statements because they contradict one another.

Clearly, there can be no such thing as an "impartial observer" of Christ's life. We have to make a choice. As Jesus tells us, "He who is not with me is against me" (Matthew 12:30).

He was born in an obscure village the child of a peasant woman... He grew up in still another village, where he probably worked in a carpenter's shop until he was thirty... Then, for three years he was an itinerant preacher... He never wrote a book... He never held an office... He never had a family or owned a house... He didn't go to college... He never travelled more than 200 miles from the place where he was born... He did none of the things one usually associates with greatness... He had no credentials but himself... He was only 33 when public opinion turned against him... His friends ran away... He was turned over to his enemies and went through the mockery of a trial... He was nailed to a cross between two thieves... While he was dying, his executioners gambled for his clothing, the only property he had on earth... When he was dead, he was laid in a borrowed grave through the pity of a friend... Twenty centuries have come and gone, and today he is the central figure of the human race, the leader of humankind's progress... All the armies that ever marched, all the navies that ever sailed, all the parliaments that ever sat, all the kings that have ever reigned, put together, have not affected the lives of men and women as much as that one solitary life.

In other words, no one could just "observe" the life and teaching of Jesus. Everyone who saw him or his disciples was forced to make a judgement. Christ was a mirror to whom people looked and saw their true selves reflected. Some people did not like what they saw, and so they hated him. Jesus himself tells us that he performed works that no one else had ever done, but still "they hated me for no reason" (John 15:25).

For others, although they did not like what they saw, this made them realise how desperately they needed him. It was these people who gathered around Jesus during his life on earth, and who formed the foundation of the Church after his resurrection.

In AD 66 Josephus, a Jewish historian, wrote: "It was at that time a man appeared — if 'man' is the right word — who had all the attributes of a man but seemed to be something greater. His actions certainly were superhuman for he worked such wonderful and amazing miracles that I for one cannot regard him as a man; yet in view of his likeness to ourselves I cannot regard him as an angel either."

The fact that Jesus is hardly mentioned outside the Gospels is not surprising. When non-Christians did refer to him, they obviously saw him as a troublemaker. The writings of two famous Romans that have come down to us illustrate this.

PLINY, writing in AD 112
In a letter to the Emperor Trajan, the younger Pliny complains that there was a slump in the agricultural markets because people were no longer buying beasts for sacrifice. This was the fault of people called "Christians", who formed a secret society and refused to offer sacrifice to the god-emperor.

TACITUS, early in the second century
The Roman historian Tacitus wrote that the Christians had been made a scapegoat for the great fire of Rome in the reign of Nero (AD 64). Their founder was a criminal who had been executed by Pontius Pilate thirty years or so earlier. Unfortunately, the death of the ringleader had not stopped the mischief!

"My words are Spirit and they are life"

Jesus is the Way

The life and words of Jesus have reached far beyond his native country and people. Followers of Jesus Christ believe his message is for all people and for all time. To understand this belief we need to look closely at the claims of Jesus himself who says: "I am the Way, the Truth and the Life."

"Where do you come from?" is a question we often ask when we meet someone for the first time. It was the question about Jesus that puzzled everyone. During his public life Jesus tried to answer that question. To those who followed him, he gave this answer,"I came from the Father and have come into the world and now I leave the world to go to the Father" (John 16:28). The Jews already possessed a deep knowledge of God. Many of Christ's sayings were already taught by the prophets and Jewish rabbis. For example, Jesus taught that when you pray you should, "go to your private room and, when you have shut the door, pray to your Father who is in that secret place and your Father who sees all that is done in secret will reward you" (Matthew 6:6).

A Jewish saying, at first glance, proclaims a similar message, "He who prays within his house surrounds it with a wall that is stronger than iron." It is important to realise that in their teachings Jesus and the other rabbis had very much in common.

The rift between them developed only gradually, as Jesus' claims became clearer. For Jesus was not just laying down a set of laws for entry into the kingdom of God. Rather, he was claiming that his presence is the kingdom of God amongst men and women. Jesus came from his Father in heaven, and his coming creates, quite literally, a heaven on earth.

The condition for sharing in this "heaven on earth" is to believe in the One whom the Father has sent; to believe in his Son and what he tells us. In Christ's own words this means "changing and becoming like a little child" (Matthew 18:3). Christ is the "Way" to the Father because his life taught us how to become "children" of the Father. This is not a "Way" which can be reduced to rules and regulations. It is a life of love. But of course the closer the intimacy between the Father and us, his children, the greater our longing to respond to all that we experience in life in the way of love: the "Way" that Jesus showed us.

Jesus is the Truth

It's always useful to have "inside information" about someone who is unfamiliar. Is that perhaps how we tend to view Jesus, someone who has come from heaven to tell us about God and what God wants us to do? What do we mean when we say that Jesus "reveals" God to us? Do we mean that because Jesus came from God, he can give us the information that we could not otherwise get?

That is not quite the picture that comes over in the Gospels. That's not the way Jesus speaks of himself. He says "I am the Truth". Not "I speak the truth" or "I reveal the truth", but "I am the Truth".

This is not to deny that Jesus had a message to proclaim and went about Palestine proclaiming it. Of course, he did. But Jesus did not only call upon men and women to believe in his message; he called upon men and women to believe in himself!

And that was something completely new. There had been prophets and teachers in the past with a message to proclaim, but none of them had demanded belief in himself. Jesus, however, slowly and gradually revealed to his disciples that he was much more than a teacher, much more than a messenger; much more than a prophet.

He had come not merely to tell men and women about God. He had not come merely as a messenger or as someone who could give us "inside information". In Jesus, God is actually made present to men and women. That astounding fact shines through everything Jesus said and did. In every word and action, Jesus reveals God to us. He shows us, in human terms, what God is like. It's as though the Father is pointing to Jesus and saying, "Look! This is the kind of God I am".

In other words, we cannot separate the person of Jesus from his teachings. Every action and gesture of his is full of meaning. He is never "off duty", there is never any moment in his life when he is not showing God to men and women.

The miracles of Jesus speak for themselves. They are an essential part of his message. Through the miracles men and women can see that the kingdom of God has begun.

Sent by his Father, Jesus does not merely *tell* us about his Father. He *shows* us his Father in everything he says and does.

" 'If you know me, you know my Father too. From this moment, you know him and have seen him.'

Philip one of his followers said, 'Lord, let us see the Father and then we shall be satisfied.'

'Have I been with you all this time, Philip,' said Jesus to him, 'And you still do not know me? To have seen me is to have seen the Father' " (John 14:7-9).

Jesus is the Life

All of us want to use and enjoy our lives to the full. But we can never forget that the greatest treasure we have, life itself, is a very fragile possession. The Jewish psalmist put it this way:

"For no man can buy his own ransom or pay a price to God for his own life. The ransom of his soul is beyond him. He cannot buy life without end nor avoid coming to the grave" (Psalm 49:7-9).

In the face of death, men and women are powerless. It was this sense of powerlessness, this awareness of their own insufficiency, which intensified the Jewish desire for a saviour.

During his public preaching Jesus said, "I have come so that they may have life and have it to the full" (John 10:10). And as time went on he began to explain to his followers exactly what he meant when he used the word "life". He told them that the only life that matters is the life that does not die – life everlasting: "I am the resurrection. If anyone believes in me even though he dies he will live, and whoever lives and believes in me will never die" (John 11:25-26).

The word used in the Russian Orthodox Church for a saint, *prepodobni*, means "very, very like" and is the means to "true life". If we want to obtain life everlasting, we must become "very, very like" Jesus himself. And we can only do this if we receive the gift of the Holy Spirit – the Lord, the giver of life.

Throughout his time on earth, the Holy Spirit worked within Jesus guiding and inspiring him. As John baptised Jesus "the Holy Spirit descended upon him in bodily form, like a dove" (Luke 3:22). And when he was led into the desert to prepare for his public preaching, it was the Holy Spirit who took him there (Luke 4:1). When he eventually began to preach in Galilee, it was with the power of the Holy Spirit (Luke 4:14).

To be really like Jesus, then, we must have the Holy Spirit within us too. That is why when the time came for him to leave his apostles, Jesus promised to send the Holy Spirit. "It is for your own good that I am going," he said to them, "Because unless I do go, the Advocate will not come to you; but if I go I will send him to you" (John 16:7).

When the Holy Spirit came to the apostles at Pentecost, they were completely transformed. The Holy Spirit bound them more closely to Jesus by making them more like him. They were filled with new life, the life of Jesus himself, and so St Paul exclaimed, "I live now, not with my own life but with the life of Christ who lives in me" (Galatians 2:20).

There is ample evidence that Jesus lived and preached in Palestine about 2,000 years ago. There is plenty of proof, too, that he was a good man. He performed miracles, and he spoke many wise words giving new hope and meaning to the lives of many people, especially those who were poor, sick or disadvantaged.

We know too, that his words and actions increasingly annoyed and threatened the established authorities of the time. They feared a public uprising, they feared loss of power, they feared the hypocrisy of their actions would be exposed. The result was that they executed Jesus of Nazareth. They hoped that his crucifixion had solved the problem of Jesus once and for all.

It seemed as though they were successful. Once dead, he was hastily buried in a tomb. They made sure that his body couldn't be removed by his followers, and then returned to the practice of their religious duties as the sabbath arrived. When the sabbath was over, some of the women who had followed Jesus went to the tomb with spices intending to complete the embalming of his body. In spite of the precautions of the authorities, the tomb was empty. It was empty, not because someone had taken the body but because Jesus had risen from the dead. Jesus was alive. It was amazing!

■ He appeared to the women: he spoke to Mary Magdalene who hurried to tell the followers of Jesus. They didn't believe her.

■ He appeared to two of the disciples who were walking to the village of Emmaus, about seven miles from Jerusalem. They didn't recognise him at first because he was the last person they expected to see.

■ He appeared to the eleven disciples as they gathered together in fear and uncertainty. They were terrified at first, thinking he was a ghost. But then they saw and touched the scars of his crucifixion, they watched him eat, and they realised he was real, a living person, raised from the dead.

Jesus had risen from the dead. Death had not destroyed him, eliminated him or removed him from the face of the earth. Jesus is alive.

In the hours after the crucifixion of Christ, his followers were a broken, lost group. This person, who had mapped out a new way of life, had offered new hope and in whom they had put all their trust by following him, was now destroyed. Their world had been destroyed. They couldn't make sense of what had happened.

Then, everything changed. Their leader who was dead is alive; he has been seen by at least sixteen people on five different occasions in different places. What does this mean? Fear is changed into hope and confidence. No one can dispute the fact that Jesus is alive.

When we face any change in life we begin to deal with it by continuing to function in the way that we have until the change. When that doesn't work any more, we face tension until we accept that our previous way of coping is no longer effective. To deal with change and to grow through it, we have to find new ways of coping, new ways of living.

The followers of Jesus ran true to human behaviour. Initially, they seem to have been happy to settle back into the pattern of simply being "led" by Jesus. But Jesus wouldn't allow that. To be a follower of Christ meant that they accepted his invitation to be part of his life and work in the world so that every person might come to know the promises of God and the surety of the resurrection and life after death.

Whenever Jesus was with any of his followers after his resurrection, he retraced with them his teaching, his words, his actions and the words of scripture. Gradually, they began to see his life and his words in a new light. Although they had been with him in his years of preaching and miracle-working, they hadn't realised the implications. They hadn't realised what it all meant.

Only on looking back, following the living proof of the resurrection, could they begin to grasp the reality of the life of Jesus of Nazareth, and the reality of what the coming of the Messiah really meant.

What makes Jesus special?

That very same day, two of them were on their way to a village called Emmaus, seven miles from Jerusalem, and they were talking together about all that had happened. Now as they talked this over, Jesus himself came up and walked by their side, but something prevented them from recognising him. He said to them, "What matters are you discussing as you walk along?" They stopped short, their faces downcast.

Then one of them, called Cleophas, answered him, "You must be the only person staying in Jerusalem who does not know the things that have been happening there these last few days." "What things?" he asked. "All about Jesus of Nazareth," they answered, "who proved he was a great prophet by the things he said and did in the sight of God and of the whole people; and how our chief priests and our leaders handed him over to be sentenced to death, and had him crucified. Our own hope had been that he would be the one to set Israel free. And this is not all: two whole days have gone by since it all happened; and some women from our group have astounded us. They went to the tomb in the early morning, and when they did not find the body, they came back to tell us they had seen a vision of angels who declared he was alive. Some of our friends went to the tomb and found everything exactly as the women had reported, but of him they saw nothing" (Luke 24:13-24).

The full significance of the death and resurrection of Jesus is hinted at in St John's Gospel. John tells us that as Jesus died on the cross a soldier pierced his side with a sword and "immediately there came blood and water". The blood and water are a sign of the outpouring of the love of Jesus. This outflow is a sign of the Spirit of Jesus in which we can all share. And then, after his resurrection, the first act of Jesus was to breathe on his followers. As he did so he said:

"Receive the Holy Spirit.

For those whose sins you forgive, they are forgiven."

(John 20:22)

In giving us his life and in sharing his Spirit with us, Jesus unites us with himself at the deepest possible level. At the Eucharist we pray to God: "Renew us by your Spirit, inspire us with your love and unite us in the body of your Son, Jesus Christ our Lord."

The work of the Spirit of Jesus Christ, symbolised so powerfully in the lifeblood and breath of Jesus, is to bring all people into harmony with God. Fifty days after the resurrection other symbols of God's Spirit were used. Christ's followers heard "what sounded like a powerful wind from heaven" and "something appeared to them that seemed like tongues of fire" (Acts 2:1-3). But whatever form the Spirit took, its effects were the same. The effect was to bring people together so that, on the day of Pentecost, everyone, of whatever language, could understand what Christ's followers were saying. When he died, when he gave himself up completely, Jesus released his Spirit in order to unite us.

In his death and resurrection Jesus released a most powerful force for the re-creation of our world. Of course, the work of the Holy Spirit will only be complete when we are all gathered together as one body in the kingdom of God. Meanwhile, we follow Christ in his struggle to bring all people to God. And we can follow Jesus in his work and in his prayer because we share in his Holy Spirit. As we will see later in *This is our Faith*, the Holy Spirit has been breathed into our own hearts so that we can show others that Jesus is alive and also share his life with others.

The work of the Holy Spirit is summarised by St Paul in his *Letter to the Romans*. St Paul tells us how the Spirit, poured out in the death of Jesus and breathed into us in his resurrection, unites us with Jesus Christ and enables us to recognise God as our most loving Father. The Spirit of God has been given to us, yet there is a struggle before the Spirit's work is complete in us and in the world.

"Everyone moved by the Spirit is a son of God. The spirit you received is not the spirit of slaves bringing fear into your lives again; it is the spirit of sons and it makes us cry out, "Abba, Father!" The Spirit himself and our spirit bear witness that we are children of God. And if we are children we are heirs as well: heirs of God and coheirs with Christ, sharing his sufferings so as to share his glory.

I think that what we suffer in this life can never be compared to the glory, as yet unrevealed, which is waiting for us. The whole creation is eagerly waiting for God to reveal his sons. It was not for any fault on the part of creation that it was made unable to attain its purpose, it was made so by God; but creation still retains the hope of being freed, like us, from its slavery to decadence, to enjoy the same freedom and glory as the children of God. From the beginning till now the entire creation, as we know, has been groaning in one great act of giving birth; and not only creation, but all of us who possess the first-fruits of the Spirit, we too groan inwardly as we wait for our bodies to be set free. For we must be content to hope that we shall be saved – our salvation is not in sight, we should not have to be hoping for it if it were – but, as I say, we must hope to be saved since we are not saved yet – it is something we must wait for in patience."

Paul to the Romans 8:14-25

The significance of the death and resurrection of Jesus

The miracles of Jesus

Throughout the Gospels Jesus is shown healing those who are sick, those with skin diseases, those suffering blindness, lameness and deafness – even raising the dead to life. It would be a great mistake to underrate the importance and the significance of these miraculous actions.

Jesus did not perform them simply to add authority to his teaching or to convince unbelievers. Nor did he perform them simply to demonstrate that he had special power. There is no hint of the show piece about them. They are not stunts performed to astonish his audience.

Far from using his miracles to impress large crowds, Jesus performed most of them in the presence of only a few people. And he frequently forbade his disciples to tell anyone about the miracles they had seen. This in itself is an indication that the miracles had a more profound purpose. Another indication is that in the *Gospel of St John* the miracles are always called signs.

Signs of what? Jesus answers that question for us, "The very works that I am doing bear witness that the Father has sent me" (John 5:36).

The miracles, in other words, are signs of his mission, signs that the kingdom of God is present and at work in the world. They are signs of God's love for men and women, signs that Jesus has come to free men and women from the sin which has brought with it death, sickness and disease.

The Spirit will teach

you everything

The resurrection of Jesus Christ struck the followers of Jesus as a burst of lightning. To begin with they were blinded. They didn't understand what was happening. They were rather like any one of us after a blinding flash or a traumatic experience. Finding ourselves in a state of shock, it takes a long time to piece together what's happened. It's a long, sometimes painstaking, process.

On their road to recovery and their search for understanding of what had happened, the first followers of Jesus enjoyed the support of the Holy Spirit, promised by Jesus. Jesus had told them:

"The Advocate, the Holy Spirit, whom the Father will send in my name will teach you everything and remind you of all I have said to you" (John 14:26).

It would be a mistake, however, to imagine that the Holy Spirit gave full knowledge and understanding to the followers of Jesus immediately. We have only to look at the followers of Jesus today to realise that we have a long way to go before we all come together as one in our understanding of and response to the words of Jesus.

It's as though the sudden burst of light at the resurrection of Jesus still blinds and confuses us. Christ's followers through the ages have struggled, and will continue to wrestle, with the full meaning of the life and teaching of Jesus Christ.

The first inspired followers of Jesus, under the apostles specially named by Jesus, continued the work and teaching of Jesus in two ways. Each of these two ways is equally important.

1 They passed on the way of life and worship given by Jesus – in the tradition of the Church.

2 They passed on in writing the revelation of God through Jesus – in the scriptures of the Church.

1. The life-giving Spirit in the Church

Following the resurrection of Jesus the first thing Jesus' disciples did under the influence of the Holy Spirit was to preach – to tell others about what had happened. Peter concludes his first sermon with the words: "For this reason the whole house of Israel can be certain that God has made this Jesus whom you crucified both Lord and Christ." As a result of his words many, we are told, were added to the number of followers.

The words of Jesus were also recalled and celebrated in their liturgy or worship. They came together for what they called "the breaking of bread" when they recalled the words of Jesus and did as he had instructed on the night before he died.

The words and work of Jesus were continued, too, in the teaching of the apostles as they faced new situations and problems. One of the most serious difficulties within the early Church, for example, was the question of Jewish observance: should all converts to the new Christian faith continue to observe Jewish customs? Such customs were a burden to non-Jews – a major source of discouragement to prospective converts. In resolving this, Peter (as a result of some pressure from Paul) took the lead. He told others: "I remembered that the Lord had said, 'John baptised with water, but you will be baptised with the Holy Spirit.' I realised then that God was giving them [the non-Jews] the identical thing he gave to us when we believed in the Lord Jesus Christ, and who was I to stand in God's way?"

Next time you go to Sunday worship take a look at the people around you. What are they like?

If yours is an average parish community your fellow worshippers will be a very mixed bunch indeed. They'll be far more varied than a football crowd or a cinema audience.

There will be people of all ages present, from babies in arms to very elderly pensioners. They will be from widely differing backgrounds: some well-to-do, others barely scraping along. There will be differences of class, race and nationality. They will have brought with them their own very different preoccupations, their problems and difficulties, their hopes, dreams and ambitions, and their fears and anxieties.

Yet the very fact that they have gathered together for worship shows that, in spite of their natural differences, there is something which unites them and which binds them together.

What binds them together is more than a belief they share, more than a common desire to praise and worship God, more than membership of a particular community.

What binds them together is not, in fact, some*thing*: it is some*one*. That truth is expressed very clearly in St Paul's greeting at the end of 2 Corinthians (13:14): "The grace of our Lord, Jesus Christ, and the love of God, and the fellowship of the Holy Spirit be with you all."

"The fellowship of the Holy Spirit..." It is here that our unity as Christians lies. For the Church is people – people united, first and foremost by the Holy Spirit who dwells in their hearts.

Sometimes when we talk about the Church we think of buildings or of a large organisation or of the bishops and other clergy. These have their place but what makes the Church to be the Church is, before anything else, the Holy Spirit in men and women's hearts.

The life-giving Spirit

Although in the Old Testament the people of God did not fully understand the nature of God, they nevertheless had a vivid awareness of the role of God's Spirit in their lives. Their understanding can best be summed up in the phrase, "life-giving Spirit".

They looked upon the Spirit as the source of all life in God's creation. But the Spirit of God was not only the source of natural life. The Jews realised, because God had revealed it to them, that the Spirit was also the source of men's and women's moral life. Those who were pleasing to God were those who had God's Spirit.

They knew, too, that God's Spirit would only be fully poured out in the world in the time of the Christ. Their experience of men's and women's sinfulness led them to the conclusion that human beings were hopelessly sinful and evil left on their own. Only when God's Spirit was poured out all over the world would things change.

The Spirit and Jesus

The Spirit of God was always with God's Son, Jesus Christ. His very conception in the womb of his mother, Mary, was, as Luke tells us in his Gospel, due to the overshadowing of Mary by the Holy Spirit of God. Jesus was anointed by the same Spirit for his saving mission as our Messiah, when he was baptised by John in the River Jordan.

Yet Jesus Christ, as a human being, could only send the Spirit to us, his brothers and sisters, when he had risen from the dead and ascended to his Father. He told us that unless he went back to his Father, the Paraclete (the Spirit) would not come.

In other words, the Spirit of God could only come upon all men and women when our leader, Jesus Christ, was re-united with his Father.

This is why the Spirit comes: to unite us to Christ and so to God our Father. The Holy Spirit, the Spirit of God, is our life. We share the life of Jesus Christ because we share his Spirit whom he sent to us.

The Spirit – the soul of the Church

Just as the different parts of our body share our life, so we and all our fellow Christians share the same Spirit, the same life of Christ. This, as we have already said, is what is meant by the phrase used by St Paul, "the fellowship of the Holy Spirit".

This, then, is the importance of the Holy Spirit: he is the ever-present source of life within us. He dwells within us, helping us to grow closer and closer to Jesus Christ. We can be confident in the reality of this if we look at the lives of the earliest disciples. Even when they had Jesus with them they were very weak in faith. In the Gospels, we see Jesus rebuking them repeatedly for their lack of faith and understanding: it's a theme which runs right through all the Gospels.

We can recall, too, their failure at the crucifixion, the betrayal of Judas who was a chosen apostle, Peter's denial, the wholesale desertion of Christ by the others. In spite of their closeness to Jesus, the weakness of their faith and their limited understanding shows up.

Yet look at what happens after the resurrection. The apostles spent the rest of their lives preaching about Jesus. They gave up their lives for him, willingly. Surely they had strong faith and a deep understanding then?

But this strong faith, this deep understanding, came to them only after Jesus had left them. What happened to transform this group of frightened, inhibited men into a force which was to take the message of Jesus Christ to the whole world?

What happened was the coming of the Holy Spirit. In fact, the apostles only fully believed, only fully understood, when Jesus Christ had returned in glory to his Father and had sent the Holy Spirit upon them as he had promised.

> "It is for your own good that I am going because unless I go, the Advocate will not come to you; but if I do go, I will send him to you... but when the Spirit of truth comes he will lead you to the complete truth" (John 16:7. 13).

At the time, the apostles couldn't understand that at all. How could any arrangement be better than having Jesus there with them? It was only after they had received the Holy Spirit that they realised what Jesus meant. Only then did they realise that, although he was no longer *physically* present, he was present in a much more wonderful way – *in his Spirit*. And that presence transformed them, they became different people.

And that presence transforms us and makes us different too. The same Spirit who came to the apostles on the day of Pentecost dwells in each one of us. It is through him that we are able to believe in Jesus Christ, love Christ and have confidence in Christ. The Holy Spirit lives in us, uniting us to Christ and pouring his love upon us. That's not simply a pious thought, we have the word of Jesus that it is a fact.

The Spirit in the Church

The Spirit doesn't just live in us as individuals. After the resurrection and ascension of Jesus, the Holy Spirit came on his followers as a body. It was in their coming together for prayer, for the breaking of bread in the Eucharist and for sharing their understanding of the life and words of Jesus that the first disciples grew in their faith in God. And the tradition that began in the teaching of the apostles continues to the present day. It may be tempting at times to "go it alone" in our faith, but it is in the community of the Church – the body of Christ – that the life of the Spirit is most certainly found.

2. The life-giving Spirit in the scriptures

As the first followers of Jesus died (many through martyrdom) they began to put down in writing their belief in Jesus. The first person to do this was Paul of Tarsus, who wrote a number of letters to his converts that survive to the present day. More importantly, others began to set down the life and teaching of Jesus in an ordered form. These books which tell us of the life of Jesus are the four Gospels. The Gospels, with the letters of Paul and a number of other writings, are known as the New Testament – the scriptures – which all followers of Jesus Christ read and revere in our growth in love and knowledge of Jesus Christ.

These two ways of continuing the message of Jesus Christ – the scriptures and the tradition of the Church – have been compared to the two streams which flow from the same source and move towards the same goal. Scripture needs to be reinterpreted in every age, but this interpretation cannot be a purely personal matter. We also need the wisdom and the authority of the Church to help us see what scripture means for us today.

It is the Holy Spirit, working in us individually and through the Church's teaching, that keeps alive the words and life of Jesus Christ. Whenever the word of Jesus is spoken or read by his followers, the power of God the Son is breathed into his followers as it was after his resurrection. It will be helpful to look more closely at how the Spirit continues to give life to the Church when Christ's followers are brought together by the words of Jesus Christ.

It is usual to read a book alone. We settle into an armchair or struggle to get a seat on a train and cut ourselves off from the rest of the world so that we can absorb ourselves in what we are reading.

It is impossible, however, properly to read the scriptures which make up the New Testament in such a way. When we read the Gospels attentively, the words of Jesus engage us and we are caught up by them. We are lifted up to a closer relationship with God. This is the work of the Holy Spirit who helps us grow in our understanding of the words of Jesus – just as the same Holy Spirit inspired their writing. As we are taken up into the life of God we are also drawn more deeply into the community of the Church that first wrote the Gospels. There is a sense in which we cannot read the Gospel entirely on our own.

The "inspiration" by the Holy Spirit doesn't mean that God dictated the scriptures aloud from heaven. God's activity always comes in a human way. He works through the circumstances of our everyday lives. And the New Testament writings, including the Gospels, were written by human beings in a human manner, but in such a way that God is their author.

Where did the Gospels come from? For the first thirty-five years after Jesus' resurrection the Gospels didn't exist. Why was that? What was happening during those first days of the Church?

As long as the apostles were still alive there was no thought of writing a book. The apostles had lived with Christ, they had known him intimately. They had seen him live, die and rise from the dead. In fact, they have been described as the "living books" on which the Christian message was written.

There were other reasons too:

■   The age in which the first Christians lived was primarily an oral one. Mass-produced printing was a long way off.

■   A single sheet of papyrus cost more than a man's daily wage.

■   The Jews and their contemporaries preferred to commit knowledge to memory rather than write it down.

Those first thirty-five years, however, were not years of inactivity, for, over this period, the Gospels were beginning to take shape in a very real way. There were three stages in this process:

Stage 1 – The life of Jesus

When Jesus was born in Bethlehem, God became human. The men and women who saw Jesus Christ saw, in a way they could understand, what God was really like. But from the beginning, he called some of his followers to be special observers, special witnesses of these important years – the apostles.

They saw him show compassion to those who were poor and those who had sinned. They saw him heal those who were sick. They heard him speak in a simple language that everyone could understand. They were the special witnesses. They knew that Jesus Christ had come to bring a message of salvation to all men and women.

Stage 2 – The preaching of the apostles

"Go out to the whole world; proclaim the Good News to all creation." The apostles were now well-equipped to carry out this last command of Jesus, and like him, they did it in a simple manner. Their intimate knowledge of Christ meant they could give their hearers a vivid picture of his life and teaching. They could describe his miracles in minute detail and repeat his stories and teaching accurately. But that was not enough. How could they best show that these stories and miracles pointed to something deeper?

Gradually, the apostles put their knowledge of Jesus into an orderly scheme. In their preaching they most probably grouped miracles together to show how everyone could share in this new life. They selected parables which urged their listeners to follow Christ. Even before the first Gospels were written, the life and teaching of Jesus was almost certainly being put into an accepted order. And this was being done by the apostles, those who really knew Christ.

Stage 3 – The evangelists

The Jewish memory was extremely retentive. We cannot easily forget repetitive TV adverts because the order of the words is always the same. The same was true of the early Jewish converts.

Once the apostles had grouped the miracles, teaching and parables of Jesus into a set order, their listeners would not easily forget. The words of the apostles would be firmly imprinted in their memory. This helps us to understand the part played by the Gospel writers.

They did not write a book in the sense that we speak of a modern author writing a book. They put into writing that which was at first passed on by word of mouth. Their work – and this is their great gift to us – brings us into direct contact with the preaching of the apostles, the official witnesses of the life of Jesus.

The two ways of continuing the message of Jesus Christ — the scriptures and the tradition of the Church — are like two streams which flow from the same divine wellspring. They are like two candles which, through the ages, continue to reveal the light which is Jesus Christ.

The calendar

Many events in life are difficult to remember. It can be hard to place them exactly in their proper order. Often it is helpful if we can arrange them round the more important events that we will never forget: was it before or after we got married? Was that the year that we went to Australia? Was that the year of the Queen's Silver Jubilee? It was a sound idea, based on that human habit, that made a monk called Denis the Little want to adjust the calendar.

Until the sixth century, events were placed in history around the date of the founding of the city of Rome. Denis wanted to change that and arrange everything round the year of Christ's birth, the most important event in the history of the world.

Denis' idea was a good one and we have become accustomed to referring to things happening "before Christ" or "after Christ". There was only one unfortunate error: Denis miscalculated the exact year of the birth of Christ. This doesn't really matter but it does mean that if we want to be precise, we would have to say that Christ was born somewhere between the years 6 and 4 BC.

Since it is known from other sources that Herod died in the year that Denis had calculated to be 4 BC, we would have to say that Christ must have been born before this. Again, if we are trying to be precise, we would also have to say that Christ probably died in the year which the calendar gives as AD 30, having begun his ministry a few years earlier.

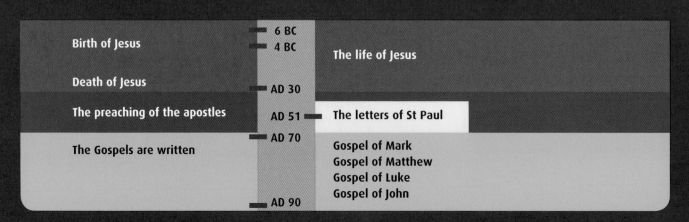

	6 BC	
Birth of Jesus	4 BC	
		The life of Jesus
Death of Jesus	AD 30	
The preaching of the apostles	AD 51	The letters of St Paul
	AD 70	
The Gospels are written		Gospel of Mark
		Gospel of Matthew
		Gospel of Luke
		Gospel of John
	AD 90	

Who were the Gospels for?

Did you know that the Gospels of St Matthew and St Mark were written with a completely different type of reader in mind? St Matthew's Gospel was written primarily for Jewish converts, while St Mark's was written for Romans. This simple fact is a strong hint to us that it is important to be careful to avoid approaching each of the four Gospels in the same way.

The Gospel of Mark

There is an early Christian tradition that Mark was a follower of St Peter in Rome. His Gospel was probably written there shortly before or after the death of Peter. It is thought that Mark's was the first of the Gospels to be written (about AD 64–67). Mark never saw Jesus so it is likely that he used Peter's accounts of the words and actions of Jesus in his Gospel.

This Gospel was written primarily for Roman converts who wanted a permanent record of the life of Jesus as it had been taught to them by St Peter. Because it was for Romans, Mark's Gospel contains many explanations of Jewish customs. It also explains the meaning of Aramaic words and expressions. The Old Testament is hardly ever quoted. Mark concentrates on Jesus as the Son of God rather than as the Saviour promised in the Old Testament.

Mark's Gospel is noted for the miracles it records. It is more a Gospel of action than of words. It is the shortest of the four and can be read at one sitting.

The Gospel of Matthew

This Gospel has been described as the greatest book ever written. It is certainly the most familiar and the most popular of the four Gospels.

Written with a fine sense of order and balance, it presents Jesus as a great teacher who fulfils the Old Testament prophecies, the promised Messiah who completes God's plan. It was written primarily for Jewish converts and therefore contains many references to the Old Testament. It was probably composed about AD 70.

This Gospel has been called the most important single document of the Christian faith because it contains the fullest account of the life and teaching of Jesus. It is also the most frequently used in the teaching and worship of the Church. Matthew was a painstaking teacher. Unlike Mark, who was often content to state bald facts about Jesus, Matthew explains at length the significance of Jesus and his teaching. Because he is speaking with a Jewish audience in mind, he plans his writing around five great discourses of Christ which are seen as the equivalent of the five books of the Torah.

The Gospel of Luke

As well as a Gospel, Luke wrote the *Acts of the Apostles*, making him the author of just over a quarter of the entire New Testament. His writings describe fully the beginnings of Christianity from the earliest moments of Christ's life to his ascension, and beyond to the years when the community of the Church was growing and spreading.

Luke is the only Gentile writer in the New Testament and it may be that this explains his interest and concern for the outsider and the care with which he records Christ's dealings with all those who were in some way outside the community.

Luke presents a picture of Christ and his teaching which has immediate appeal even on the human level alone. His Gospel was primarily intended for Christians already familiar with Gospel teaching, but it also seeks to attract non-Christians. It was written in Greek and has an educated style. It emphasises that Jesus is the Saviour of all women and men, and stresses the compassion of Jesus for the poor and the outcast. It has been called the *Gospel of social justice*.

The Gospel of John

The Gospel of John shows a marked difference from the other three Gospels. All four evangelists select their material to suit their purpose but this selection is most evident in John. John's Gospel was written in Greek about AD 90 and bears the characteristics of an old man's reflections on past events, delving into their deeper meaning. The purpose of this Gospel is "that you may believe that Jesus is the Christ the Son of God..."

Although John's Gospel carefully places events in a thoughtful order, it would be a mistake to think of it as straight reporting. With this Gospel, more than the others, we have to read between the lines for the full meaning. It is one of the most inspiring parts of the New Testament and one of the best loved. This is partly due to the fact that it is a very personal statement of faith in Christ. John the Evangelist knew how to transmit his own living memories, and his love for Christ is obvious on every page.

The Church has always reverenced this document as the work of John the Apostle, although the Gospel as we have it would appear to be the work of his disciples who actually wrote down what John had taught and dictated.

The Spirit for our wounded world

Once the followers of Jesus realised, having encountered their risen Lord, that Christ really was the Son of God, they were facing a new and serious dilemma: how would they cope with this information? How would *anyone* cope with such information? It was great news, exciting and encouraging, but it was also overwhelming. They were ordinary people, not scholars, religious or unusually gifted. What could they do with the Good News they knew to be true?

One of the important points of the Good News is, of course, that God is in control of his world; he knows what is best for his people. And so, true to his word, God acts. Christ, in his appearances after his resurrection, helped his followers to make sense of what had happened:

"He then opened their minds to understand the scriptures, and he said to them, 'So you see how it is written that the Christ would suffer and on the third day rise from the dead.'"

He reassured them that a change of heart (repentance) would ensure a new beginning,

"And that in his name [Christ], repentance for the forgiveness of sins would be preached to all the nations, beginning from Jerusalem. You are witnesses to this" (Luke 24:45-48).

And finally, he promised that he would be with them always,

"Go, therefore, make disciples of all the nations; baptise them in the name of the Father and of the Son and of the Holy Spirit, and teach them to observe all the commands I gave you. And know that I am with you always; yes, to the end of time" (Matthew 28:19-20).

"As the Father sent me, so am I sending you" (John 20:21).

The Father sent his Son into the world to show us once and for all the true nature of God – that he is a God of love. That Spirit of God which had been with Jesus in his life on earth is promised to all who believe and accept the Good News of the true nature of the kingdom of God. They will never be alone because the Spirit of God will be intimately involved in all that they say and do in his name. This is how the kingdom of God is formed on earth: by those actions of the Holy Spirit in and through the people of God.

What's the matter with our world?

Original sin

St Paul tells us of the existence of original sin in his letter to the Romans. Original sin is the basis for all sin in the world. It is the foundation of the absence or denial of God in the lives of men and women.

In Genesis, we read the story of Adam, the first man, a representative of the human race. As our representative, Adam was created holy and a perfect example of a complete and just human being. But Adam chose to follow his own choices, his own ways, rather than the ways of his creator. His will was superimposed on the will of God and so disorder, death and deterioration entered the world.

In sending us his Son, Jesus Christ, God offers to all men and women a chance of a new creation. A creation which is once more holy, just and eternally life-giving. Jesus Christ revealed the healing, guiding hand of God in our world; offered it to all who would accept it. Pride, the desire for self-worship and a rejection of God's ways, recurs, but we know that we are not expected to overcome these hurdles, these hardships, alone.

Jesus Christ told us of the kingdom of God. He told us the Good News that we are redeemed, sanctified and made one with our heavenly Father in and through our baptism.

In baptism we are plunged into water which symbolises the watery ferment of the story of creation, but also reminds us of water as a source of life. The baptismal font represents the womb, symbolically fertilised by the paschal candle, from which our new life is born; new life, infused and guided by the Holy Spirit. All who are baptised share in this life of God promised by Jesus Christ.

Clearly, in spite of this new birth, we are still inclined to sin and self-worship. We are still drawn towards turning inwards and focusing on our own values and desires. As long as we live, we rely constantly on God's healing Spirit to renew us, restore us and to help us overcome our failings to live our new life as a true reflection of Christ's life.

The magnetic pull of original sin remains with us as long as we live, but the grace and strength of the Spirit of Christ are always powerful enough to overcome it. We are dependent on God. We are created and we exist through his loving creativity. All life and love is a gift. In living in unity with God we find a completeness which is not to be found elsewhere. That is our faith. That is Christ's promise. Original sin no longer has any power over us as long as we acknowledge our dependence on God.

What's the matter with our world?

We can put people on the moon; we can fly the Atlantic in a few hours; we can watch events on the other side of the world as they happen. In the field of technology men and women have made tremendous progress. But when it comes to the business of living together in peace, of caring and loving, we seem to have made little or no progress at all. In some respects, the ways in which we hurt and destroy one another seem to have got worse. At times it can feel as though we are going backwards not forwards. And the really numbing thing about the evil we see all around us is the feeling that we, as individuals, can do little or nothing about it all. We feel helpless.

What's the matter with us?

Yet the disease is not only in the world around us, it is also in ourselves. We, too, do our share of harm to others. We are selfish and cruel. We fail to love, day in and day out.

The inescapable conclusion is that there is something wrong with men and women. Somehow, somewhere along the line, we got involved with sin. There is no need, at this point, to look back at the beginnings of human history to find out precisely how we got into this situation. The important point is that this situation is a fact. It is plain for all to see.

If we have any doubts about our world's need for redemption, for a fresh start, we need look no further than today's news bulletin. If we have any doubt about our own personal need of redemption, we need look no further than our own hearts.

Why did Jesus come?

"The Son of Man has come to seek out and save what was lost." The idea of being "lost" is a very good description of what sin means. When we are lost we have left the right road; we're wandering aimlessly with no sense of purpose or direction.

Wars, massacres, cruelty, exploitation, race hatred, injustice, crime... Our newspapers and TV screens are full of all these things. We can't get away from them.

Men and women turned away from God are lost. They have broken off contact with God who alone gives meaning and purpose to life. They become rather like the airline pilot trying to land in fog, having lost contact with ground control. Unable to re-establish contact, the pilot only wanders further and further away from the true destination.

If men and women are to find their way again it must be shown to them. We must be put on the right road once more. This can only be done by someone who knows the way, someone who has not lost contact; someone, in other words, who knows no sin, whose vision is clear and unclouded.

Jesus came to do that for us. He came to re-establish for us a true and loving relationship with God, his Father. Through Jesus it becomes possible for us to break out of the net of sin in which we have become imprisoned.

A shattering truth

Jesus, as he himself said, came to seek out and save what was lost. That simple phrase contains a profound truth, a truth which stands at the very heart of the Christian message: the truth that God gives himself to us.

It is men and women who have failed. It is men and women who have destroyed the relationship between God and themselves. But God does not wait for the guilty to come to him to be reconciled. God goes out to them. God gives himself to them. God, in Jesus, seeks them out.

And there are no strings attached. No conditions laid down. God, quite simply, gives himself to men and women: a free gift of himself.

This shattering truth sets Christianity apart from other world religions. It stands our usual way of thinking about religion on its head. Men and women have always thought that they must remove the guilt they feel before God by their own unaided efforts, thinking that they must do something in order that God will look kindly on them.

The truth is almost exactly opposite: God already looks kindly on them. This is overwhelming. So overwhelming that when they heard this, when they heard that God had given himself to men and women, many did not accept him.

Why does God allow suffering in the world?

This is the commonest objection to belief in God and there is no slick answer to it. A starting point is to ask, "What sort of world would it be in which suffering was totally eliminated?" Clearly it would be a very different world from the one we live in now. First of all, the physical environment would have to be different. A world in which, for example, there could be no earthquakes, no drought, no floods, no disease would have to be a physically different world from the one we live in. Is such a physically different world possible? Modern science seems to suggest that it isn't. The basic laws of physics are so finely tuned that even a minute change in them would reduce the world to chaos. If this is the case then it looks as though the laws which make it possible for us to exist at all are the same laws which create the conditions in which suffering is possible.

But even if the physical world could be changed so as to eliminate the possibility of diseases and natural disasters, that would not solve the problem. There still remains the suffering which human beings inflict on themselves and on each other. To change *that* would mean changing *people*. Their freedom of choice would have to be destroyed, for people cannot have true freedom unless the possibility of misusing it is there.

Would it be a better world if we had no free choice, if we were all programmed automata? Would such an existence, with all suffering eliminated, be worth having?

Suffering, then, seems to be a consequence of the way things are. But it would be a mistake to think that God is indifferent to suffering, or worse – that he deliberately inflicts it. We believe that God has revealed himself in the person of Jesus Christ. And in Jesus Christ God has subjected himself to the consequences of the universe he has created. When Jesus died in terrible agony on the cross he showed himself to be at one with suffering humanity. He also showed that suffering can be transformed into life, that evil can be overcome by love. This helps us to glimpse the meaning of suffering: that it is not all a futile waste.

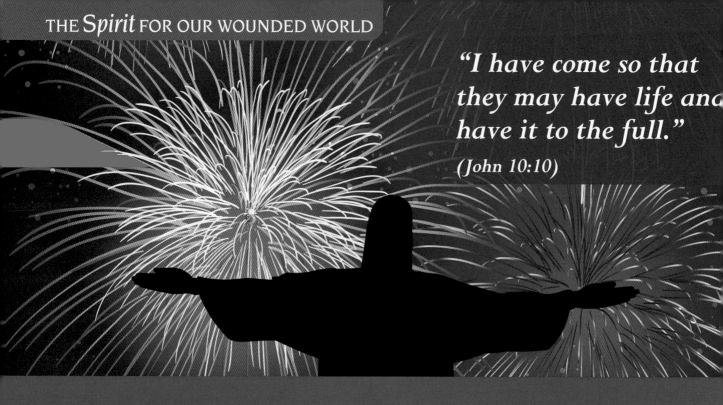

> *"I have come so that they may have life and have it to the full."*
> *(John 10:10)*

What did Jesus do for us?

Jesus made it possible for us to stop being the kind of people we are and to become the kind of person he was, the kind of person we were created to be: a reflection of our heavenly Father. That is what redemption means.

- ▨ Jesus lived in the world as one of us.

- ▨ He was fully human and fully divine.

- ▨ He shared with men and women the human condition which involves suffering and death.

- ▨ But where others sinned, he remained sinless.

- ▨ Where others failed to love, he loved completely, unconditionally.

- ▨ Where others did only their own will, he carried out the will of his Father.

In everything he did, Jesus showed us what it means to live with and for his Father. Jesus, though, did not come simply as an example which we could follow. He did not come simply to be the perfect model of someone who lived a fully human life as God intended it to be lived. He came to make it possible for us to overcome the suffocating power of sin. He came to make it possible for us to change.

Jesus made it possible for us to change by his death and resurrection. We can never hope to understand that fully and that's why we speak of the *mystery* of our redemption. All we can do is to try to get as near the truth as possible.

Why did Jesus die on the cross?

In trying to understand the answer to this question we must reject, right from the start, any false idea of God the Father as a harsh and cruel judge who demanded that his Son should suffer and die to make up for the sins of men and women. It is love, not some abstract idea of justice, which provides the key to our understanding.

"God loved the world so much that he gave his only Son, so that everyone who believes in him may not die but have eternal life. For God did not send his Son into the world to be its judge but to be its saviour" (John 3:16-17).

Jesus suffered because suffering is an inevitable part of human existence: no one is free from it. He suffered, too, because what he was, what he taught and what he did, provoked resistance and hostility from sinful people. It was men and women who refused to accept Jesus and his teaching, men and women who put Jesus to death.

Jesus could have avoided the cross, he could have run away, but he didn't. Instead he remained true to his Father, true to the message of love which he had come to bring. In other words, he remained faithful to his Father's will and his faithfulness brought him to death.

Where does the resurrection fit in?

When Peter and the other apostles received the gift of the Holy Spirit at Pentecost and started to preach the Good News of the Gospel, the central point of their message was the resurrection of Jesus from the dead. The resurrection is the basis of our Christian faith. Why is it so important?

It would be a mistake to think of the resurrection merely as a proof that Jesus was God. The significance of it goes much deeper than that. St Paul gives us some idea of its significance when he says, "... if Christ has not been raised, you are still in your sins".

The resurrection is the completion of the sacrifice Jesus made on the cross. Because Jesus remained true to his Father's word, his Father raised him from the dead to a new life of glory. Jesus is reunited with his Father for ever. And because Jesus is our our older brother, our representative, he has reunited the fallen human race with God. Our redemption, our new beginning, is achieved.

Jesus – the light of the world

There is nothing so discouraging as being told constantly to "try harder". Our driving instructor tells us to "try harder" and we find ourselves driving into the lamppost instead; we "try harder" to be patient with someone whom we find difficult and end up saying the worst possible things. Being told to "try harder" generally ties us up in knots as we wrestle with our weaknesses and anxieties.

One of the consoling things about Jesus is that he never told us to "try harder". He never said that, in our lives, we needed more effort. However, he did tell us that, in our lives, we needed more light. That is why he invites us to follow him in his path to happiness. For Jesus' vision of that path is clear and unclouded. In following him we see life in a new light and this, more than anything, will change our behaviour and the way we act.

What are the principal ways in which our ways of thinking and acting are changed in the light of the teaching of Jesus Christ?

■ The teaching of Jesus shows us that religion is not a set of laws but is a relationship. It is always tempting to reduce religion to rules. Some rules are an essential part of any human society and Jesus himself emphasised the importance of the Law in providing us with boundaries for our behaviour. The relationship between God and ourselves, however, like the relationship between parent and child, is not founded on rules but on trust or what Jesus calls "faith". Rules and laws can never be a substitute for faith. Jesus came among us, above all, to open our eyes to God's trust in us and assures us that true happiness is to be found in placing our faith in him.

■ The teaching of Jesus shows us the dignity of each one of us. This is an area where so many people live in darkness – they are blind to the beauty of themselves and of others. For example, Jesus reminds us how God clothes the wild flowers growing in the field which are there today and thrown into the furnace tomorrow so, "will he not much more look after you, you who have so little faith?" He tells us, "see that you never despise any of these little ones... it is never the will of your Father in heaven that one of these little ones should be lost." And Jesus reassures us that those who follow his word are not his "servants" but "friends" who live in the same love of the Father as he himself.

This puts our understanding of the dignity of ourselves and of others in a wholly new light. This is why the Church places such importance on the dignity of every person from the moment of conception to the moment of death. It is the basis of the Church's insistence on the importance of individual conscience and the responsibility we have for informing it, for conscience is the "still small voice" of God within us, prompting us to follow his will.

■ The teaching of Jesus gives us a sense of direction and purpose. Without help and training, a blind person will bump and bang into every obstacle in his or her path and be badly hurt. Similarly, without the light of God's word we will damage each other and the world in which we live. Light enables us to see where we are going. And so Jesus tells us:

"I am the light of the world; anyone who follows me will not be walking in the dark but will have the light of life" (John 8:12).

In the light of the words of Jesus every action of ours takes on new meaning. Each action contributes to the building up of the kingdom of God in this world and moves us towards God, who lives in eternal light. And so we can look forward to the day when, at last, we see God face to face and enjoy true happiness for ever.

At the beginning of his Gospel, John refers to the "darkness" of this world (John 1:5). Jesus himself was often to refer to it and, at the hour of his death, we are told that "darkness came over the whole land until the ninth hour... when Jesus had cried out in a loud voice, he said, 'Father, into your hands I commit my spirit'" (Luke 23:44).

Jesus certainly did not escape the sin and suffering of this wounded world. He was crucified by it. Yet in his life and at the moment of his death he shed light on the way to a solution. In the giving up of his Spirit which is released for every person to share, he invites us into a new relationship with his Father, he helps us to recognise the dignity of every person and he gives us new purpose. This new vision proclaimed by Jesus Christ is infinitely more effective than any attempts on our part to "try harder" in the reconstruction of this world and the building up of the kingdom of God.

The Spirit of God has made a home in you

Throughout his life and his teaching, Jesus makes it very clear that God is our deeply loving parent who longs for a full and complete relationship with us, founded and centred upon mutual love and confidence. God already knows all our needs, all our weaknesses, our hopes and our fears. God is on our side, God is close to us and God loves us. Prayer has been described as "wasting time with God" and that is a very good description of it. Just as two lovers are happy to spend time together simply enjoying one another's company and presence so, too, in prayer we grow towards that kind of relationship with God.

That doesn't mean that we shouldn't speak to God in more basic ways like giving thanks, asking for help and expressing our sorrow for sin and failure. But it is important that we don't let our prayer life stop there. Why? Because it is only through developing our closeness with God that we become more like Jesus Christ and so become a true reflection of his love in our world and in our relationships.

"The Spirit too comes to help us in our weakness. For when we cannot choose words in order to pray properly, the Spirit himself expresses our plea in a way that could never be put into words, and God who knows everything in our hearts knows perfectly well what he means, and that the pleas of the saints expressed by the Spirit are according to the mind of God" (Romans 8:26-27).

In prayer we meet God. We learn to see the world and other people through God's eyes. We begin, too, to see ourselves with God's eyes and learn to understand what it means to be loved sincerely and unconditionally for ever.

Jesus tells us about effective prayer

"I say to you: Ask, and it will be given to you; search, and you will find; knock, and the door will be opened to you. For the one who asks always receives; the one who searches always finds; the one who knocks will always have the door opened to him. What father among you would hand his son a stone when he asked for bread? Or hand him a snake instead of a fish? Or hand him a scorpion if he asked for an egg? If you then, who are evil, know how to give your children what is good, how much more will the heavenly Father give the Holy Spirit to those who ask him!" (Luke 11:9-13).

The prayer of Jesus

In the great prayer of Christ following the Last Supper, which is recounted in St John's Gospel, Jesus takes his followers to the heart of the meaning of his life and of his death which is to follow on the next day. In this prayer, Jesus shows us that prayer is at the centre of his and of our relationship with the Father.

In this prayer, Jesus glorifies his Father and gathers up all who follow him into that prayer. He prays for those who have heard his words and believed in him. He prays that in their unity with him, they may discover a unity amongst themselves, so that all may be one, united in Christ and so united with his Father in heaven.

In this unity, they will share in the redeeming work of Christ and in the suffering which he is to undergo. But in sharing that suffering they also share his glory. All who are faithful in unity with Christ will share the glory and joy of the resurrection. In all this they are to be faithful not only to the words of Christ but also to his way of the cross, to his way of unconditional love for their fellow men and women. Christ prays for his followers and will continue to pray for them; he will protect them and he will consecrate them to himself through his prayer always.

Prayer, then, unites us with Christ and with his Father so completely that the world will know that Christ was from God in our faithful reflection of his life and death.

First steps in prayer

Many of us find the road to prayer hard going. This is often because our approach to prayer is determined by a primitive view of God.

So many of us have not really listened to Jesus Christ telling us in his parables about the true nature of God. He speaks of the prodigal son; the host who invited everyone, even the most miserable beggar, to his table. Yet we cling, in spite of everything, to the image of a God who is ever ready to avenge and punish us. Small wonder that we often find it a grim and nerve-racking experience to talk to such a God in prayer.

The apostles weren't afraid to ask Jesus to teach them how to pray. He knew their weakness and gently set them on the road to prayer. Many have travelled that same road since and their experiences form part and parcel of the rich tradition of the Church.

It's impossible to outline here all the advice and guidance of so many men and women. But it is clear that there are certain steps which can help us develop a rich and authentic prayer life.

1. Prayer is a meeting

We cannot allow ourselves to forget this. Prayer is a meeting with God. It is not some magic formula for disciplining the mind. Neither is it a soothing way of escaping from the pressures and worries of life. First and foremost, prayer is a meeting with our heavenly Father and if it is to be a real meeting, we must take the second step...

2. Be yourself

We've all heard of the sad clown who hides behind the smiling mask. All of us have a wardrobe full of masks and we can use them as well as any quick-change artist.

The tragedy is that as long as we have our mask on, nobody ever meets us. They meet the highly professional business man, the skilled worker, the home-loving mother, but they never see the insecure, anxious, sad clown that we really are. What a relief when we can reveal our true self to someone who loves us.

God loves you. God loves each one of us. It's easy to be ourselves with him. Once we try this we find we have taken the second step in prayer. But if this meeting is to be a success, there is something else we must do...

3. Let God be God

It rarely strikes us how arrogant we are. We're like the child who told his mother he was about to draw God. "But no-one knows what God looks like," he was told. "Not at the moment," he agreed, "but they will when I've finished."

We think we know God and understand God. Somewhere in an old attic of our minds we store a picture of God and keep on bringing it out like some dog-eared photograph from the family album.

Yet there is a truth we cannot avoid. No man or woman can fully understand the creator of all things. God is completely beyond our understanding. We have to learn to throw away all our preconceived notions about God and let God come to us as he really is, not as we would have him. Then we are ready to take one more step forward...

4. Give God your worries

"Come to me all you who labour and are overburdened and I will give you rest... " As long as we hang on to our worries we will have to carry a burden which is so unwieldy that it obscures our vision of God.

It's important that we take God at God's word and give God all our worries. Once we start trusting him it's amazing how relieved we begin to feel. It's like taking a heavy haversack off our backs after a long gruelling walk.

Once this barrier has gone, we are ready to talk to God. We can use set prayers if we wish to, or simply talk to him naturally if we are able to do so. Alternatively, we can simply sit in companionable silence with God. This leads us to a final step...

5. Listen

An old saying comes straight to the point: "God has given you two ears and one mouth that you may listen to him twice as much as you speak to him."

It's easy to ignore the obvious but a conversation is not only talking, but listening. It is important for us to be silent and listen to our God speaking to us. More than that, we must let Jesus Christ speak through us. He will if we give him the chance. And when he does, we will:

"With all the saints have strength to grasp the breadth and the length, the height and the depth; until, knowing the love of Christ which is beyond all knowledge, [we] are filled with the utter fullness of God" (Ephesians 3:18-19).

Jesus tells us how to pray

"In your prayers do not babble as the pagans do, for they think that by using many words they will make themselves heard. Do not be like them; your Father knows what you need before you ask him. So you should pray like this:

Our Father in heaven,
may your name be held holy,
your kingdom come,
your will be done,
on earth as in heaven.
Give us today our daily bread.
And forgive us our debts,
as we have forgiven those who are in debt to us.
And do not put us to the test,
but save us from the evil one.

Yes, if you forgive others their failings, your heavenly Father will forgive you yours; but if you do not forgive others, your Father will not forgive your failings either" (Matthew 6:7-15).

Starting meditation

Some people find that meditation is the form of prayer, the way of communicating with God, which they feel helps them grow closer to God. A simple form of meditation revolves round a single word or a short phrase which is repeated steadily and rhythmically. The name "Jesus" has often been used in this way, either by itself or as part of a longer phrase. For example, during the season of Advent a suitable phrase to use would be "Come, Lord Jesus".

The purpose of this phrase (sometimes called a *mantra*) is twofold. First, it occupies the surface of the mind, aiding concentration, clearing away distractions and helping to bring peace and stillness.

Second, it carries a power of its own. As one writer has put it, "The mantra, repeated and repeated until it is engraved on the tablets of the mind, has incredible motive power; it can heal, it can transfigure, it can transform."

Now here's an easy step-by-step guide to this form of meditation:

1 Find a place where you can be alone and undisturbed for the period of meditation – say between ten and twenty minutes.

2 Take up a firm but comfortable position – sitting up straight in a chair or cross-legged on the floor.

3 Lay your hands on your lap or on the arms of the chair. Close your eyes and relax.

4 Spend a few moments in silence, breathing gently and rhythmically.

5 Begin to say the phrase "Come, Lord Jesus," over and over again (in your mind rather than out loud). Say it slowly. You may find that after a while the words coincide with your breathing. This is a further aid to attentiveness, but don't try to force it.

Remember, the aim isn't to achieve anything or to experience anything. It's simply to be still and at peace, attentive to the presence of God in the depth of our hearts.

Always the same Spirit

Some time ago, a parish priest wrote to every parishioner explaining that the annual cost of heating the church was several thousand pounds. He pointed out that, although it wasn't a large church, the roof was twenty metres high. To overcome the problem of costs, the building was to be weatherproofed as much as possible and he suggested that people dress more warmly, remembering that centuries ago churches weren't heated at all. "But," he continued, "the best way that parishioners can help is to bring a friend to church with them; for body heat is still our most precious natural energy resource."

The priest's suggestion was offered "tongue in cheek" but it was an obvious one. On average, the heat from three people is equivalent to a one-kilowatt electric fire. It is so easy to overlook the obvious. We can spend so much time building and repairing beautiful churches and constructing all kinds of efficient organisations for the running of the church and end up giving no energy to the love – the warmth – that alone gives life to God's Church. A small congregation worshipping in a ramshackle building and willing to share their lives – even sharing their body heat – is far more certain to survive and grow than a mass of people sitting comfortably in a church kept cosy by central heating and so able to keep their distance from each other.

The beginning of the Church goes back to that day when the first followers of Jesus came together in a room to support each other. In the *Gospel of John* we are told that "the doors were closed in the room where the disciples were, for fear of the Jews" (John 20:19). Then Jesus breathed on them and gave them his Spirit. In the *Acts of the Apostles* we have a more complete picture of what happened.

Again, it was after the resurrection of Jesus when his followers were still unsure of what was happening.

"When Pentecost day came round, they had all met in one room, when suddenly they heard what sounded like a powerful wind from heaven, the noise of which filled the entire house in which they were sitting; and something appeared to them that seemed like tongues of fire; these separated and came to rest on the head of each of them. They were all filled with the Holy Spirit and began to speak foreign languages as the Spirit gave them the gift of speech" (Acts 2:1-4).

The writer of Acts then goes on to say how Peter, the leader of the apostles, told the people in Jerusalem about Jesus: how he had died and risen again, and how new life and the Spirit of Jesus were offered to all who acknowledged him. "That very day," we are told, "about three thousand were added to their number."

Today, that there are over a billion followers of Jesus Christ in our world. Although growing larger by the day, the group of Christ's followers remains essentially unchanged. This assembly is known as the Church, from the Greek word *ekklēsia*, meaning "an assembly called together".

The Church, then, is not a building. It's a gathering of people. And although each one of us is unique, we are held together by the Spirit of Jesus who lives within each one of us, drawing us closer to God and to each other, and who enables us to acknowledge Jesus as our Lord.

When Jesus spoke about the future of his followers, he painted certain characteristics which, today, are summarised in the Creed which we say at the Eucharist. We profess our belief in "one, holy, catholic and apostolic Church". It will be helpful to look at each of these in turn.

The Church is one

This means that we are united in the life of God. Jesus spoke of himself as a vine: "I am the vine, you are the branches. Whoever remains in me, with me in him, bears fruit in plenty; for cut off from me you can do nothing" (John 15:5). The Spirit of God who unites us is like the sap in the vine: normally we can't see it, yet it gives life. And the proof that we are alive is that we bear fruit which refreshes and nourishes the world in which we live.

The Church is holy

Jesus, the Son of God, shared his life with us wholly. And he promised that he would continue to do so. "If anyone loves me," he said, "he will keep my word and my Father will love him, and we shall come to him and make our home with him" (John 14:23). Jesus is "at home" with us. Our lives can, and so often do, bring others to God.

The Church is catholic

This means that the Church embraces all peoples in every age. The final command of Jesus was to "go and make disciples of all nations and baptise them in the name of the Father and of the Son and of the Holy Spirit" (Matthew 28:19).The Church, then, is not an exclusive club for those we happen to regard as suitable. It is for everyone.

The Church is apostolic

It is God who calls us together as a Church. But we remain human beings. The Church is formed by God as an organisation built upon human beings and, in particular, on the apostles and their successors, the bishops. We know from the Gospels that the apostles were far from perfect. Yet it is so often in human weakness that the power of God becomes most evident.

The Church is people

Jesus certainly had to deal with a great deal of weakness from his own closest followers. One of the apostles, Philip, said to Jesus on the night before he died, "Lord, let us see the Father and then we shall be satisfied." It was with some exasperation that Jesus replied: "To have seen me is to have seen the Father" (John 14:8-9). A few years later St Paul said the same thing using different words. He described Jesus as "the image of the unseen God" (Colossians 1:15) and "the revelation of a mystery kept secret for endless ages" (Romans 16:25).

These words, "secret" and "mystery", have very similar meanings and they give us the word "sacrament". (This word "sacrament" comes from the Latin word "sacramentum" which was used to translate the Greek word for "mystery".) Both Jesus and Paul were emphasising the same truth: if we want to see what God is like then look at Jesus himself and hear what he says and see what he does.

And today, now that Jesus has returned to his Father, if we want to see what Jesus is like we are to look at his Church and hear what the Church says and see what it does. Sometimes we refer to Jesus as the "sacrament" of God; and we refer to the Church as the "sacrament of Jesus Christ". "From the side of Christ," the Church tells us, "came forth the wondrous sacrament of the whole Church."

It is impossible to overemphasise the closeness between Jesus Christ and the Church. The very first act of Jesus after his resurrection was to breathe on the apostles in the small room where they had gathered together for comfort, and to give them his Holy Spirit. But Jesus looked beyond that room to the end of time and prayed to his Father that all people would come together and forgive each other so that "they may all be one".

"Father," he prayed, "May they be one in us, as you are in me and I am in you, so that the world may believe it was you who sent me"(John 17:21).

The Church, then, is the people who come together as one to share in the goodness of God and to celebrate it. Each time we assemble we gather in the warmth of God's love. The little room in which Jesus first appeared has been enlarged to take in the whole world and every age.

The Church and the Trinity

The life of God – the life of the Father, the Son and the Holy Spirit – is at the heart of the Church's life and teaching. Jesus, the Son, confirmed our belief that God is not unmoved or unconcerned by human beings and that God loves us deeply. Jesus Christ told us that he was wholly one with the Father and that he sends his Holy Spirit to unite us with God.

We refer to the doctrine of the Holy Trinity as a "mystery". The "mystery" of the Trinity is not primarily to do with how the one God exists in three persons. The "mystery" of the Trinity is primarily about relationships – the perfect relationship between the Father, the Son and the Holy Spirit.

This is difficult to understand because we're not very good at relationships. We're better at using our intellect and, over the centuries, our fund of knowledge has increased dramatically. At the same time, however, our ability to enter into happy relationships hasn't improved at all. The first experience of man and woman was a sense of loneliness and isolation. Such loneliness continues to cut across wealth or power or status.

It may be obvious but it is a truth worth repeating, nonetheless, that God did not involve himself with humankind because God was lonely and bored. The Son, Jesus, didn't come among us for a "chat" as we might go to our neighbour for a cup of coffee. For the Father, the Son and the Holy Spirit enjoy a perfect relationship. They do not suffer loneliness. Their happiness and the love between them are perfect and complete. And we say that the relationship between them is a great mystery, not because it is a truth about which we can know nothing but because it is a truth about which we can never know everything. Our relationship with God can never be complete in this life because we're not very good at relationships. And so the mystery of the Trinity is beyond us.

There are certain truths about the Trinity that we can learn, however. A good relationship is always based on loving – on giving. And each person of the Trinity has been given to us in a particular way. We recognise the Father in particular as the origin of creation and of re-creation. "God loved the world so much," Jesus tells us, "that he gave his only Son."

And the Son, Jesus, is the person of the Trinity who united himself with human flesh in order to reveal God's love. The penalty he paid was a painful death because the world wasn't interested. He gave himself to us in flesh and blood; as he continues to give himself, under the form of bread and wine, in the Eucharist.

And the Holy Spirit, finally, is the third person of the Trinity who comes into the world every day to draw us into the love of God. The Spirit is the love of God who draws us to the Father and to one another. Jesus called the Spirit the "Comforter". The Holy Spirit is usually regarded as the expression of the mutual love between Father and Son: similarly the Spirit is the bond of love between the Father and humankind. The Spirit enables us to cry out, "Abba, Father", which is the cry of the child entering into a perfect relationship with the heavenly Father.

To understand these relationships within the Trinity and to enter into their mystery is more than the work of a lifetime: it is the work of eternity. For we are not talking about a mathematical formula or a scientific analysis in which, at the end of our search for a solution or answer, we can experience the joy of crying out: "I've solved it", or "I've discovered it". We are talking about relationships. And in a relationship there is always room for growth.

As our relationship with God does grow we begin to overcome our loneliness. We begin to enter into a communion far more profound than a purely human community. We enter into the life of the Father, the Son and the Holy Spirit.

The holiness of the Church?

The Church tends to get a bad press these days – not only from people outside but also from critics within its own ranks, particularly among younger members. Critics often concentrate on the Church as an institution; and institutions, they say, are cold, heartless things, ever ready to stamp on anyone who steps out of line. But it's not only the institution that comes in for criticism. Attention is also drawn to the many Christians who clearly fail to live up to their Christian ideals.

The Church accepts the failure of its members

Criticisms like these are fully justified. The Church itself freely acknowledges that it is far from perfect. All Christians, clergy and lay people, remain sinners. Even a great saint like Paul acknowledged he was only an "earthen vessel", and that so often when he wanted to do good his human nature won out, and he found himself doing wrong despite himself (Romans 7:15-25).

Yet, while acknowledging that the Church has many faults and failings, we also maintain that the Church is "holy". Isn't that something of a contradiction? We say that the Church is holy but in fact the Church doesn't really look all that holy.

How can this be resolved? First of all, by realising that when we speak of the holiness of the Church, we are not speaking primarily of the holiness of its members but of the holiness of Jesus Christ. Through the Church the holiness of Jesus Christ becomes present among men and women.

That holiness is a gift, freely given through the power of the Holy Spirit who dwells in the hearts of all Christians. So, every Christian carries within him or her the holiness of Christ.

The holiness of Christ is offered to all in the Church

Clearly this holiness ought to be reflected in the life of each individual Christian: it ought to be expressed in a life of goodness, a life of love and service, modelled on Jesus himself. Some Christians do achieve this: they are the saints of the Church – canonised and uncanonised. But for most of us it's a different story. We often fail to live up to the gift we have been given; we ignore or reject the murmur of the Holy Spirit within us.

It is here that we see again the amazing extent of God's love. In spite of our failure, in spite of our faithlessness and sinfulness, God, through his Spirit, continues to give himself to us. He's ready to welcome us again and again, to make us holy in spite of ourselves and our foolishness.

This should not surprise us. For while Jesus was on earth he mixed freely with sinners and the outcasts of society. In doing so he showed us what true holiness is: not judgement and condemnation but redeeming love.

The Church continues the redeeming work of Jesus. The Church must, therefore, draw sinners to it and offer them – through the proclamation of the Gospel and the celebration of sacraments – the holiness of Christ. This the Church continues to do, no matter how much Christ's holiness may be obscured by the failure and sinfulness of individual members.

The Anglican Church and church unity

It seems that there was never a time when the Church did not suffer from divisions. Only about twenty years after the resurrection, St Paul had to write a warning to the Christians in Corinth, where some were saying, "I am for Paul", others "I am for Apollos", others "I am for Cephas". "Is Christ divided?" Paul asks, reminding them that the Church must be one united body (1 Corinthians 3:1-9). And John's Gospel tells us that Jesus prayed for the unity of the Church at the Last Supper, on the night before he died: "Father, may they all be one. May they be one in us as you are in me and I am in you, so that the world may believe it was you who sent me" (John 17:11. 21-23).

The first big and lasting split within the mainstream Church itself came in 1054 when the bishops of the eastern part of the Church, centred on Byzantium, and the western Church, centred on Rome, were unable to heal the divisions that had grown up between them as a result of living separately for centuries. These eastern churches, strongest today in Greece, eastern Europe and Russia, are known as the *Orthodox* churches.

The second big split came with the Reformation in the sixteenth century, when Protestants, claiming the Bible as their primary authority, also separated from Roman Catholicism and set up independent churches with various patterns of ministry and government. Since the Reformation further splinterings have occurred, so that there are now very many Protestant denominations with different teachings.

The Church of England also separated itself from the Pope's authority at the Reformation, though like the Eastern Orthodox churches and some Lutheran churches, it kept a Catholic structure organised around the ministry of bishops, priests and deacons, and retained some Catholic teachings and practices that Protestant churches generally abandoned. This Catholic inheritance of the Anglican Church was further emphasised and strengthened in the nineteenth century by what is sometimes called the Anglo-Catholic or Oxford Movement.

At the Reformation, Anglicanism also adopted much of the Protestant insistence on the importance of scripture, personal faith, individual conscience and evangelism. This inheritance is especially emphasised by the Evangelical movement within the Anglican Church. Because of this dual influence, the Anglican Church stands between the churches of the Reformation on the one hand and the Roman Catholic and Orthodox churches on the other – a sort of Reformed Catholicism.

By now Anglicanism has spread all over the world especially to those countries which were historically most closely associated with England. Today the Anglican Communion consists of over 30 national churches. The Archbishop of Canterbury, however, remains a focus of unity for the whole Anglican Communion and presides as Chairman of the International Conference of Bishops.

As a church which combines a Catholic and Protestant inheritance, Anglicans have a special reason to appreciate and value the riches of Christ in all Christian traditions, and to work for the reconciliation of the differences that still divide us.

As St Paul wrote, "There is one Lord, one faith, one baptism" (Ephesians 4:5). Happily, most of the main Christian churches – Protestant and Catholic – recognise one another's baptism, and accept that by baptism we are all members of Christ's one body, whatever denomination we belong to. In other words we are all members of the one "invisible" Church of Christ, even if we belong to different "visible" churches. But we still have to pray, as Jesus himself prayed, that the "invisible" unity may become a visible reality and a witness to the world.

The origin of sacraments

When Jesus died on the cross his disciples were confused, frightened and unsure of their future. In the days following his resurrection they gathered together for mutual support and to try to make sense of what was happening.

As they gathered together, Jesus came amongst them. He was different from the Jesus they were familiar with and yet they recognised him and knew him in his words and in his actions.

In listening to his words, they began to see more clearly and understand more fully who he was and what his message meant. His vision and his teaching about life, which he had shared with them when he was with them before his crucifixion, were now in sharp focus. As they listened to his words, they recognised him as the Son of God: they knew he was indeed the Christ.

In witnessing his actions in the resurrection, in the breaking of bread and in the sharing of himself, they came to share the reality of his faith, his unity with his heavenly Father, and an understanding of his responsibility and love for all men and women.

The disciples experienced the action and the power of the Holy Spirit in and through this unity with Jesus Christ and with each other. As a result of this they gained in confidence and courage to move out from that frightened, nervous group, hiding away in a "safe" meeting place. They moved out into the world to share in turn what they had received: mutual support, the word of God and the experience of the Spirit of Jesus in transforming and renewing life.

This pattern has remained essentially the same in the life and work of the body of Christ – the Church – from the earliest days until now.

At the heart of the life of the Church are the sacraments which constantly renew and reconcile the Church to God. And the celebration of every sacrament follows that original pattern experienced by that very first community of believers following the resurrection:

- Christ's followers gather together as a community.

- This community listens to the word of God.

- The community shares the experience of God's action.

- They depart to serve others and bring them the Good News.

It is clear from this pattern that being a follower of Christ is not simply a private arrangement between God and the individual. The opposite is true. Being a follower of Christ means being part of a community, part of the Body of Christ here on earth, today. In becoming part of that Body we don't lose our own individuality, rather we become more fully ourselves because we are accepted as free to be what God has created us to be. And we accept others on the same basis because in our baptism we are united in God and in God's love and care for every other person.

It is only when we are afraid to show our weaknesses, afraid of what others may do to us or afraid of being ignored, that we move into the false security of isolation.

Jesus came to free every person from such isolation. He came to make us truly free and, in his life, he showed us the reality of what being human really meant. Being truly human means being Christlike. Anything which prevents that makes us a less than fully human being.

Holy oils

In the Old Testament, oil had a significant role for the people of God. Oil penetrates deeply into the body giving strength, health, suppleness and beauty. It's not surprising, then, that to be anointed with oil was a sign of rejoicing and respect. In the Old Testament, too, we read of anointings taking place as part of rites of consecration. The outward significance of these anointings was that the anointed one had been chosen by God to be God's sign to the people. A king so anointed became a sharer in the Spirit of God.

"Christ" means "anointed one" for Jesus was given a special work to do. He suffered and rose again in order to unite us to his heavenly Father. A Christian, as a reflection of Christ, also has special work to do in living as a member of Christ's body, the Church, and in revealing him to other men and women. For this reason, "anointing" with oil plays a significant part in our celebration of the sacraments as a sign of being an "anointed one".

On Maundy Thursday in most dioceses the bishop blesses the oils which are to be used for anointing during the year ahead.

These oils are then distributed to priests for use in their celebration of the sacraments with their local Christian community.

Three oils are blessed:

- ☐ Oil of Catechumens or Oil of Baptism is used for anointing new members of the Christian community. It is olive oil.

- ☐ Oil of Chrism which is used as a sign of sealing with the gifts of the Holy Spirit and is used when a profession of faith is made at baptism, confirmation and at the ordination of priests. This oil is a sweet-smelling mixture of olive oil and balsam.

- ☐ Oil of the Sick which will be used to anoint those who are sick and those who are dying. This oil is a sign of healing of body, mind and soul. It is olive oil.

The creative Spirit
The sacrament of baptism

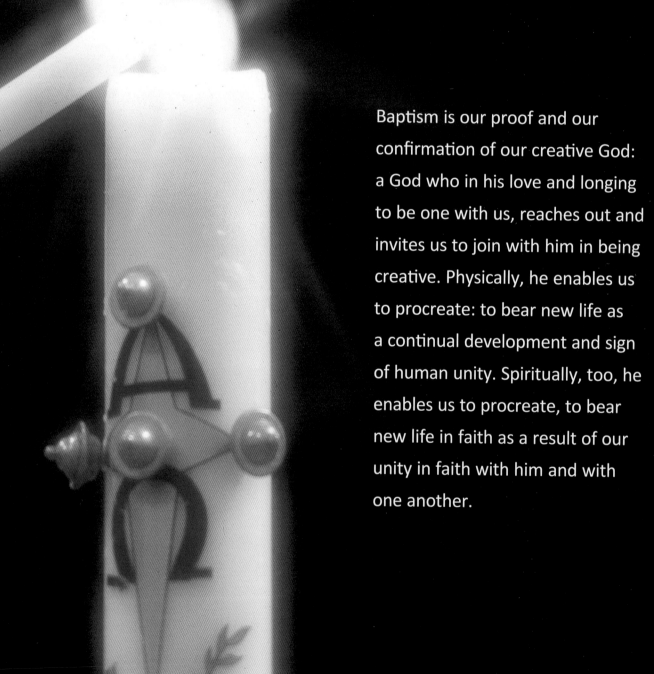

Baptism is our proof and our confirmation of our creative God: a God who in his love and longing to be one with us, reaches out and invites us to join with him in being creative. Physically, he enables us to procreate: to bear new life as a continual development and sign of human unity. Spiritually, too, he enables us to procreate, to bear new life in faith as a result of our unity in faith with him and with one another.

Infant baptism: our beginning not our arrival

A baby's baptism is simply the start of a life of faith. It is a welcome into the community of God's people, who want to help the baby to understand and share in what being loved by God means. Baptism is God's token to us of his great love – it's a love token. In all sacraments faith carries us forward to the sacrament, but when we are babies it is the faith of our parents and the Christian community which carries us to the sacrament. It follows, then, that to fulfil the true meaning of the sacrament, and to achieve the authenticity of the sign of baptism, there must be continuing teaching and example of living faith.

It's easy to see, then, that what happens *after* baptism is vitally important if we are to experience the fulfilment of the promise of this fundamental sacrament.

What difference does infant baptism make?

At baptism, we join God's family and become a baby Christian. As with most things in life, being baptised won't necessarily make much difference to us unless there is further input. Being baptised is the *beginning* of something, it is not an isolated event or a magic moment which acts like a good luck charm for life. Jesus Christ asks us to baptise in his name so that parents, godparents and God can work together in a creative partnership throughout the crucial years ahead as we grow to maturity.

For the first nine months of life, a baby lives in the womb totally dependent on its mother for life and nourishment. After birth, a baby continues to be dependent on its mother and the immediate family for continuing care for many years until he or she is mature enough to live as an adult.

A baby only grows, and will only continue growing, as long as the care, protection and guidance needed to reach successful maturity continues to be given. In the same way, a baby Christian will only grow and continue to grow as a Christian if there is support, example and teaching throughout childhood and adolescence. By bringing their child to be baptised, parents are giving a sign to the world that they and God are indeed partners working together for the complete development of their child – body and soul. As with other aspects of growing up, if support and encouragement are not given, or are withdrawn too early, permanent immaturity is the result. It's not always too difficult to spot that amongst ourselves as Christians.

Our faith makes a creative difference

It's very difficult to be a member of a family if you never have any contact with other members of the family. And it's very unreasonable to expect people to bring up a child as a Christian if they're not trying to live as Christians themselves.

For these reasons, the Church is more concerned than ever today that parents who ask for their child to be baptised also understand what is involved and understand what their commitment and responsibilities will be concerning the growing faith of their child.

Often parents ask for baptism for their baby because they think it's a nice celebration or the family or grandparents say that the baby must be baptised. It may be that they think of baptism as a special kind of blessing which will safeguard the child. All these reasons are very understandable but they are not the heart of baptism.

Most parents who bring a baby to be baptised do so because they want to share their own faith. If the faith of the parents is less certain, then the Church community needs to willing to be that baby's Christian family. Baptism brings them into this family of God. Being part of a family means growing up in the ways of that family. It means belonging, learning, sharing, in a certain way of life. That is the meaning of baptism: it's a sign of the beginning of life as a Christian.

What is the point of baptising a baby if he or she will not be able to grow and develop within the family of God? If parents don't regularly practise their faith, they cannot be expected to be able or willing to pass it on to their child. In that case, the Christian community where the baby is baptised might like to nominate their own "godparent" for the baby, someone who will go on praying for him or her, and keeping in touch, as a representative of the baby's Christian family. Our faith is a creative relationship with God, and the Church community can play a vital role in baptism.

The creativity of God – baptism is our invitation

God created us with great love. God wanted us to exist, God wanted us to be part of his creative life. Since our baptism, our beginning of life in and with Christ, we may have lost sight or perhaps forgotten God's creativity in our life. Whatever has happened to us, whatever the quality of our relationships with the Church and with other Christians, God continues to invite us to share in his creativity.

What is baptism?

Baptism means "plunging". Jesus was baptised in the River Jordan by John. The sign of the Holy Spirit was seen, and the Father's voice was heard, "This is my Son, the Beloved; my favour rests on him" (Matthew 3:17).

Jesus called his death and resurrection a "baptism". To his apostles he said, "Are you willing to be baptised with the baptism with which I must be baptised?" In this baptism Jesus was "plunged" into death but the Father raised him up in the power of the Holy Spirit.

Baptism is the sign instituted by Jesus to unite us with his own baptism. What happened at Jesus' death and resurrection is what happens at baptism, so that St Paul could write, "When we were baptised in Christ Jesus we were baptised in his death; in other words, when we were baptised we went into the tomb with him and joined him in death, so that as Christ was raised from the dead by the Father's glory, we too might live a new life" (Romans 6:3-4).

Baptism is a sign of salvation because it is the sacrament introduced by Jesus to make us part of his Body, the Church. Jesus told Nicodemus, "I tell you most solemnly, unless a man is born of water and the Spirit, he cannot enter the kingdom of God" (John 3:5).

Godparents

In the earliest days of the Church, the sponsors at the baptism of a child were the parents. But more commonly, the baptisms in those days were of older candidates, so this was often not possible. Many parents of converts could not or would not stand as sponsors.

Slaves were without their parents, and many younger children had been abandoned by their parents and had been taken in by the Christian communities. Very often sponsors at these baptisms were deacons or deaconesses. Only one sponsor was required; in the case of adults they had to be of the same sex as the candidate. These sponsors were called "spiritual parents" and their duty was to give instruction both before and after baptism and to be a guardian of the spiritual life of the baptised person. This is the origin of the term "godparent".

Today the role is secondary in the case of infant baptism. If necessary, godparents should be ready to help in the spiritual education of their godchild. It's important that godparents are sufficiently mature (usually over 16) and are aware of the responsibility they are taking on, so that they can conscientiously promise to help bring the child up in faith. A parent should not be the only godparent to his or her own child.

Water

Water is a sign of cleansing. The baptismal water used with the prayers, calling on the Father, the Son and the Holy Spirit, cleanses the one being baptised of original sin and all actual sin committed before baptism.

Water is also a sign of new life. The newly-baptised is given the new life of the Holy Spirit which unites the person in the life of the Trinity. We call this new life "sanctifying grace".

The Christian name given at the "Christening" is a symbol of the truth that the newly-baptised person belongs to Christ and is made like him.

What are the effects of baptism?

Baptism gives us the character of Christ. This is like the impression made by a parent on their child; it is permanent and irrevocable. St Augustine compared the baptismal character to the mark or seal tattooed on a soldier to show who was his lord. When the sacrament is celebrated God gives himself to us. Therefore, this sacrament never needs to be repeated.

Because baptism confers the character of Christ, it gives the one who is baptised a share in Christ's priesthood and the power therefore to worship. This is the reason why a person must be baptised before being able to celebrate any other sacraments.

What happens at baptism?

▣ Baptism is generally celebrated at a public service, most appropriately at the Eucharist, the Church's family meal. But it may also be celebrated at another separate service.

▣ The ceremony begins with a welcome to all who come for the baptism from the priest or minister on behalf of the Christian community, the Church.

▣ There is a pause for prayer. Then we listen together to the word of God and are invited to respond in faith.

▣ The person is beginning a journey of faith and the priest reminds the child's parents and godparents: "You speak for them today. Will you care for them and help them to take their place within the life and worship of Christ's church?"

▣ The decision: this is expressed emphatically in a threefold rejection of evil and a threefold affirmation of Christ the Lord.

▣ The priest may now make the sign of the cross on the baby's forehead. Parents, as well as godparents and sponsors, may also be invited to sign the baby with the sign of the cross.

▣ Gathered at the baptismal font, we are reminded of the significance of water in the history of God's people and now in the sacrament of baptism. Baptism signifies the new life won for us when Jesus rose from the dead. The congregation are invited to profess together the faith of the Church.

▣ Now comes the climax of the whole ceremony as the priest or minister dips each candidate in the water or pours water over the forehead saying: "(N), I baptise you in the name of the Father and of the Son, and of the Holy Spirit." To which all answer in faith "Amen".

▣ The newly baptised person may now be clothed with a white robe, to symbolise being "clothed with Christ". The oil of chrism may be used, signifying that the child is anointed like Christ.

▣ We pray especially for parents and godparents who have the prime responsibility for guiding and helping the child.

▣ The congregation expresses its joy: "We welcome you into the fellowship of the faith; we are children of the same heavenly Father; we welcome you." The priest introduces the peace and may invite all to exchange a sign of peace.

▣ Finally, the priest or another person may give the new Christian a candle lighted from the large Easter candle: "You have received the light of Christ; walk in this light all the days of your life."

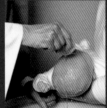

Conversion and adult baptism

Conversion

Conversion literally means "turning round" – which is why the first question the candidate is asked at baptism is, "Do you turn to Christ?" When we become a Christian, we stop drifting with the way of the world and start swimming against the current – with Christ as the new direction of our lives. Sometimes this change happens dramatically, as when Paul was converted on the Damascus road. For most of us it happens slowly, often after a long period of experience and thought. But always it is the work of the Holy Spirit in us, prompting us to see in Jesus the meaning and goal of our life, and to commit our lives to him.

In recent years, as the number of young children baptised has tended to decrease, the number of unbaptised adults seeking baptism has tended to increase. The situation is becoming more like that of the early centuries of the Church, when the Church's growth came mainly through the admission of adults.

The ancient rite of admission to the Church

In the oldest pattern of Christian initiation, adults were prepared over a long period, sometimes of some years. Entry to the Church normally happened at Easter, and during the season of Lent immediately before it the candidates' preparation was at its most intense. The climax came on Easter Eve, when the candidates were baptised, and then confirmed immediately afterwards. So, baptism and confirmation were originally part of a single rite of adult initiation. After confirmation the new Christians, clothed in white, were admitted to the altar and received communion for the first time at the Easter Eucharist. The ceremony was timed and designed dramatically to underline that it is by baptism that we are made members of Christ's body, the Church, and so united to the mystery of his death and resurrection.

The separation of baptism and confirmation

It was only when the baptism of children became normal, around the fourth century, that, in the western part of the Church, baptism and confirmation were separated. Parents and godparents now made the baptismal promises on behalf of baptised infants, and confirmation was reserved to a later stage when the child had grown up and could answer for himself or herself.

These days, adults can sometimes feel embarrassed to ask for baptism, because it has come to be associated with babies in popular thinking. But it is important to remember that originally it was normally intended for adults. It also means, of course, that it does not make sense for an adult to seek baptism without also intending to receive the second part of Christian initiation in confirmation, and to receive communion as a practising member of the Church. So when an adult seeks admission to the Church, first there is a period of instruction and preparation, which will vary according to the individual. Then, when the candidate is ready, baptism, confirmation and first communion are normally administered together at the same service, as happened originally – though the service is no longer restricted to Easter.

Can someone be re-baptised?

Many have been baptised as children, or even confirmed, but real faith fails to flower in them. They have never felt it "on the inside", it has never become a reality for them, so they may even declare themselves atheists or agnostics. But then, in later life, suddenly or slowly, a real and living faith dawns upon them, and they may ask for re-baptism or re-confirmation, feeling that it "didn't work", as it were, the first time.

Baptism and confirmation, however, are once-and-for-all sacraments. They cannot be undone or re-done. They remain effective pledges even if the fruit of faith is not immediately apparent after them, because God always leaves us free to accept or reject the grace God freely gives. If someone has only been baptised before the light of faith dawns, the appropriate way of declaring one's new commitment would be to seek confirmation. If baptism and confirmation have already been received, a person can renew their baptismal vows in church, and can also ask to confess their failings and receive forgiveness before joining the people of God at the Eucharist. Sometimes, too, provision is made for a public profession of faith and commitment.

Committed Christians are usually very busy people. They are involved in lots of things: they have a lot to do. Committed church people seem to be involved in so many activities and organisations: they support parish activities, they support the schools, they support moral and civil rights organisations. They are also involved in church synods, committees, lay ministry, worship, teaching, and social and fundraising activities. It would be easy for an onlooker to think that to be a "real" church member means you have to have an extra shot of energy and drive for all worthy causes. Unfortunately, many people's image of the sacrament of confirmation reinforces this idea. All too often confirmation is seen as the sacrament of Christian action or the sacrament of becoming a "Soldier of Christ". All of these ideas and images can be very misleading.

Confirmation celebrates the presence of the Holy Spirit within us

Our confirmation is, then, a continuance of what has begun at our baptism: a continuance of the developing awareness and reality of faith, and the presence of the Holy Spirit in our lives. At our baptism, faith was conceived, we became part of Christ's body – part of his Church. The Holy Spirit ensures that we are a brother or sister of Christ. Our confirmation is the gentle unfolding of what our baptism means.

When we celebrate confirmation, we celebrate the fact that we are being transformed, and that transformation

will continue to take place from the day we are confirmed until we are completely one with God. We are on a journey to wholeness, peace and perfecting love. We can celebrate that. Our heavenly Father celebrates with us because we are responding to his invitation to a life of love and reconciliation. We have said "yes" to his invitation to be part of the visible, living, breathing, Spirit-filled body of Christ. It is only through the action and lives of Christians that the Holy Spirit, through faith and the sacraments, can show what the Church is truly called to be: the living body of Christ. And this must be at the heart of any other activity we undertake.

The gifts of the Holy Spirit

There is an ancient tradition in the Church of speaking about the *seven gifts of the Holy Spirit*. The custom can be traced to Isaiah 11:1-3 and it sets down the following gifts:

■ Wisdom: The power to see all things as God sees them.
■ Understanding: The gift of understanding God's revelation.
■ Counsel: Helps us to see just what we should do in a difficult situation.
■ Inward Strength: The power to carry through joyfully what we know to be right.
■ Knowledge: The gift of knowing the truth; knowing the Father and Jesus the Saviour whom he sent among us.
■ True Godliness: Leads us to feel for God the love that a child feels for a loving parent and enables us to see all others as our brothers and sisters.
■ Fear of the Lord: Enables us to be willing to respond to the impulses of the Holy Spirit, and gives us a fear of being separated from God.

It is important to remember, though, that being a Christian is the first gift of the Holy Spirit, and that each person has special gifts that the Holy Spirit uses for the good of the whole Church.

The living Spirit
The sacrament of confirmation

What is confirmation?

During the life of Jesus and after his death and resurrection, his followers grew to know and love him. They began to see in his teaching an answer to the questions and problems they encountered in their lives. Once they had witnessed his resurrection, they became completely convinced that they wanted to remain his followers for the rest of their lives. Just before his ascension, Jesus told them to spread the message of the Good News he had brought to them to the whole world. He then promised that he would be with them always (Matthew 28:20). The significance of this promise failed to register with them until Pentecost, the day when the disciples were filled with the Holy Spirit. Then, suddenly, they had the courage to speak out, strength to begin building a Christian community and an amazing power to convince others of the truth of what they said about Jesus Christ.

It is this strength, courage and power that is the Spirit of Christ. Jesus was true to his word: he hadn't left them, his Spirit came into their hearts, permanently. This same Spirit enters our lives in this active way at our confirmation.

From the earliest days of the Church, the gift of the Holy Spirit has been linked to baptism. In the *Acts of the Apostles*

we read how Philip the deacon made converts in Samaria and baptised them. The apostles then sent Peter and John to the converts. On arrival they prayed "for the Samaritans to receive the Holy Spirit, for as yet he had not come to any of them: they had only been baptised in the name of the Lord Jesus. Then they laid their hands on them, and they received the Holy Spirit" (Acts 8:15-17).

Later, when Paul came to Ephesus, he found disciples who "were never even told there was such a thing as a Holy Spirit". They had received only John's baptism. When they heard of Christ, "they were baptised in the name of the Lord Jesus, and the moment Paul laid hands on them the Holy Spirit came down on them, and they began to speak with tongues and to prophesy" (Acts 19:1-6).

In each case, baptism was followed by the laying on of hands. Just as Jesus had invited his followers to join him, it was only after they had received the Holy Spirit that they were able to go out and pass on the Good News about the kind of life Jesus had revealed to them. So it is with us: we receive the invitation and accept it at baptism. This is followed by "the laying on of hands" at confirmation which inspires us to preach the Gospel.

The Spirit of life

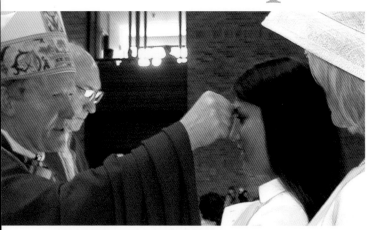

A popular children's party game – for parents as well as children – is Dead Lions. It's especially useful when things seem to be getting out of hand. Everyone lies flat on the floor pretending to be dead, there must not even be a flicker of life. Meanwhile, the person who is "it" tries to spot any movement, laughter or breathing. The great advantage is that it provides about three minutes of peace! For those who are supposed to be "dead" its disadvantage is that it is almost impossible to lie "dead" still. Suddenly, we become aware that even our breathing, usually unnoticed, is ruining our chances of staying in the game.

Breathing is like that – we forget about it most of the time, but at every key moment in life we watch anxiously for it. At birth, however well the baby looks, however smooth the delivery, we dare not relax until the first breath is drawn. And then, at the end of life, we wait with bated breath ourselves for the final breath; and when there is no more breathing we cannot believe the silence.

In confirmation we are confirmed in the Holy Spirit. The Holy Spirit is the breath – the life – of God. And it is given to us. We share the life of God.

And in this breathing of God's life into our own souls we are given the gift of tongues just as the apostles were given it. For in the Holy Spirit we receive God's love which gives us the power to love as God loves. And love is a common language to all people. Love unites: we can speak to all men and women in all nations in this universal language which says, "You matter... you are of infinite value."

Much of the time as Christians we play Dead Lions with our heavenly Father. We just don't move as Christians, we fail to reveal the gift given to us in confirmation; we fail to breathe in the life of the Spirit. Yet we know that to give up breathing altogether is certain death. In every effort we make, no matter how small, to follow Christ, we are already responding to the breath of the Holy Spirit – the language of love. And that language of love, received at our baptism and confirmation, is the breath of eternal life which God continues to share with all who choose to follow the way revealed to us by Jesus Christ.

"The gift of the Holy Spirit closes the last gap between the life of God and ours... When we allow the love of God to move in us, we can no longer distinguish ours and his; he becomes us, he lives in us. It is the first fruit of the Holy Spirit, the beginning of our being made divine" (Austin Farrer).

What happens at confirmation?

▨ Those to be confirmed, their family, friends and the local Christian community, gather together, usually at the Eucharist.

▨ The candidates are presented to the congregation and they may give a short testimony of faith.

▨ The candidates renew their threefold baptismal decision rejecting the powers of evil and affirming their faith in Christ.

▨ The bishop extends his hands over those to be confirmed and prays that they will be given the sevenfold gifts of the Holy Spirit.

▨ In some churches, the Oil of Chrism is used and the bishop makes the sign of the cross on the candidate's forehead.

▨ The bishop addresses each one by name: *(N), God has called you by name and made you his own.*

▨ Then the bishop lays his hands upon the head of each one saying: *Confirm, O Lord, your servant with your Holy Spirit.*

▨ The bishop then invites the whole congregation to pray with him this solemn prayer: *Defend, O Lord, these your servants with your heavenly grace, that they may continue yours for ever, and daily increase in your Holy Spirit more and more until they come to your everlasting kingdom. Amen.*

▨ Those newly confirmed are invited to share in Christ's mission building the kingdom of God. Finally, all exchange the sign of peace, symbolising the fellowship and unity of all in full membership of the Church.

Living the Christian life

Being a Christian means that "making a fresh start" is always possible. The Holy Spirit guiding us and prompting us gives us confidence and courage to face our failures and to try again to follow Christ. When Christ appeared to his followers after his resurrection his first words were, "Peace be with you." Later, he promised to send the gift of the Holy Spirit to them to make that "peace" possible. There are five key points to living as a Christian:

1 Accept change: Jesus said, "Unless you change and become as little children you cannot enter the kingdom of heaven." Most of us prefer a cosy existence in which we are disturbed and bothered as little as possible. And we prefer it when God leaves us alone. If we are going to enjoy new life then we have to leave that old life behind. It means accepting a God who enters into our lives totally. And so we have to want to follow Christ perfectly and experience the happiness and peace which only he brings. If we really want to become a Christian and are prepared to pay the price for it and have our life upset as a result, then we have made the first step on the way to our own resurrection.

2 Accept your own failings: Sins and failures are not, in themselves, a barrier to God. The barrier is a stubborn heart and will in which we say to God, "Keep away". Jesus didn't keep away from the company of sinners but only from the proud. The life and work of Jesus is full of his consolation for those who have fallen and lie in defeat. Our God is the God of those who fail. This doesn't mean that God loves failures more than others but simply that God helps them more because God sees and understands their need. St Paul once made the extraordinary statement: "If I am to boast, then let me boast of my own feebleness." Paul's realisation of his own weakness was the moment of truth in his own spiritual struggle; and the Lord reassured him,"My power is at its best in weakness." Our consciousness of weakness gives God room to work. Pride alone makes God powerless.

3 Accept the failings of others: This means realising first of all that others are like ourselves; and secondly, that they have a right to our forgiveness just as God forgives us. The alternative is far more damaging for us than for them. For our refusal to forgive means taking on the burden of hate. As Martin Luther King once wrote, "I've seen too much hate to hate myself... and every time I see it, I say to myself, hate is too great a burden to bear..." One of the first conditions of prayer is a forgiving heart. Clara Barton, founder of the American nursing profession, never held a grudge. Once a friend reminded her of something cruel that had been done to her but she seemed not to remember it. "Don't

you remember the wrong that was done to you?" the friend asked. "No," Clara replied, "I distinctly remember forgetting that."

4 Keep an eye on God: St Francis de Sales tells us that we are always to be like very small children going for a walk along a country lane. They cling with one hand to their loving parent while they gather blackberries with the other. If we ask our heavenly Father to hold us in his arms all the time we will remain as babies. But if we hold on to him with one hand while we gather and handle the things of this world with the other, we are free to turn to him from time to time to see if he is pleased with what we are doing. To let go of our heavenly Father altogether on the pretext of gathering more will result in our stumbling. Prayer is the way of keeping our attention fixed on God, and short, frequent prayer from the heart is far better than attempting long and laborious prayers from a book. In prayer, it is God's Holy Spirit at work in us who leads us.

5 Keep one eye on others: When we are locked away from others we often become lonely. And loneliness can lead to self-pity. Giving even a cup of cold water to others reminds us that we have something to give and so have something to be grateful to God for. Once, there was a grieving woman who visited a holy man in China and asked him to help her overcome her sorrow. He told her she must obtain a mustard seed from a home that had never known sadness and it would banish her sorrow. The woman couldn't find such a home. Instead, wherever she visited, she was told of the tragic things that had happened there. On hearing each tale she asked herself, "Who is better able to help these people than I, who have known so much sorrow?" She became so involved at easing the grief and comforting others that she forgot about her search for the mustard seed which, in fact, had driven the sorrow from her life.

The nurturing Spirit
The sacrament of the Eucharist

The Eucharist helps us to make sense of our world. To an onlooker it may seem that what happens at Eucharist bears little relation to what's going on in the world; it seems irrelevant. But Christians see the Eucharist differently. We believe that what happens at the Eucharist is really a picture of what is happening in the world. The Eucharist is like a lens which brings into sharp focus those things that we often overlook. Through this lens, we can see the true nature and meaning of our world and the reason for our existence. By looking at what happens at the Eucharist we begin to see the world in a new way. So let's look more closely at what happens at the Eucharist...

Coming together

The first thing we see is people coming together. They come from different homes and situations: some happy, some sad, some fulfilled, some lonely. But there is a unity. Church people are united in that we believe that coming together for the Sunday Eucharist, or Mass, or Holy Communion is important. For we believe that, despite all the problems, God's power is at work in the world and that God's strength can overcome human weakness. This is true for people of every race, colour and creed. Our coming together as Christ's followers brings into focus this belief in God's power within each one of us.

Listening

The second thing we see at the Eucharist is that very soon everyone sits down to listen to the scriptures being read. There are a lot of ways in which we believe that God has spoken and continues to speak to people. Human experience and our own conscience, for example, are ways in which God touches everyone. Yet for Christians there is something more: there is Jesus Christ and all that he has taught us about the Father and his love for his people. That's why, at the final reading, which is from the Gospels, we stand to listen to the words Jesus himself spoke. When we listen to God's word in the scriptures it brings into focus God's voice in the world.

Thanksgiving

The third thing we see as central to the Eucharist is what we call the "Eucharistic Prayer". The word "Eucharist" comes from the Greek word meaning "thanksgiving". Everyone gathers around the altar with the priest to re-enact what Christ did with his disciples at the Last Supper. We listen afresh to Christ's words thanking and praising God saying, "Take, eat; this is my body which is given for you; do this in remembrance of me." Then, "Drink this, all of you; this is my blood of the new covenant, which is shed for you and for many for the forgiveness of sins. Do this, as often as you drink it, in remembrance of me."

We believe what Christ said. We believe that when we remember and act on his words, Jesus is present. This is the most precious moment of life. The bread and wine which have been brought forward to represent our life and work now become for us the Body and Blood of Jesus Christ. He is present, as he said he would be, and is our reminder of God's unending promise. But this precious moment doesn't mean that what's happening in the rest of the world is irrelevant. The opposite is true. This moment reminds us of the importance of every single person in God's eyes. Our celebration of Christ's presence among us brings into focus just how precious the whole of God's world is.

Communion

Finally, at the heart of the Eucharist, is Holy Communion. This is a personal moment. When we share in this sacred meal we do indeed share in the life of Christ. We are experiencing the result of God's great desire to come to us and be one with us. To make the bread and wine for our communion, grapes and grain are crushed. Jesus Christ was also crushed for our communion. He was crushed and crucified on the cross, so that the power of God's love for all could be shown. In all our lives there is suffering, but our suffering is not meaningless. For, when suffering is faced with love, that which is crushed and broken is transformed by such love into new life. Our celebration of communion brings into focus the cost of all true loving and shows us where such love will lead us – into the hands of God, the creator of love.

What does the Eucharist tell us?

When we think about the reality of what our celebration tells us, it becomes clear that in the Eucharist we find all that we need in life. We find unity with others, guidance from our heavenly Father, food for the journey and confirmation of the promise which was made to us by Jesus Christ. The Lord has not the slightest intention of leaving us to our own devices and our narrow outlook on life. Having created each of us to be special and unique, he doesn't leave it there any more than we would leave a newborn baby to fend for itself. No, our heavenly Father intends to nurture and cosset us every moment of our lives until the day we are completely one with him in love, unity and peace.

God gives us his Body and Blood as a sign of God's continued presence and to nurture and continually form us in God's likeness. We are called to bring Christ to our home, our workplace, our world. And we are called to do this, not by hollow words and empty gestures, but as Christ comes to us – in a simple, everyday way, a gentle way with ordinary, everyday gifts and actions which transform and nurture in a profound and authentic way.

Early Days

From the earliest days the Christian community has come together to celebrate the Eucharist. The *Acts of the Apostles*, written around the year AD 70, tells how the early Christians met regularly for "the breaking of bread" (Acts 2:42). And in one of the most valuable documents we possess, Justin the Martyr gives us this unique picture of the celebration of the Eucharist in AD 150:

"On the day which is called Sunday, all, whether they live in the town or the country, gather in the same place.

Then the memoirs of the Apostles or the Writings of the Prophets are read for as long as time allows.

When the reader has finished, the president speaks, exhorting us to live by these noble teachings. Then we rise together and pray. Then as we said earlier, when the prayer is finished, bread, wine and water are brought. The president then prays and gives thanks as well as he can. And all the people reply with the acclamation, 'Amen'.

Then the eucharistic gifts are distributed and shared out to everyone, and the deacons are sent to take them to those who are absent."

The Eucharist is a mystery which touches the life of the whole world. It is like an irresistible magnet which in the huge sprawling cities and the remotest villages stirs people out of their homes and groups them together around the Lord. The language can be different, the external shape and form can change, but the essence of the mystery remains always intact. Nothing has changed since Justin's day.

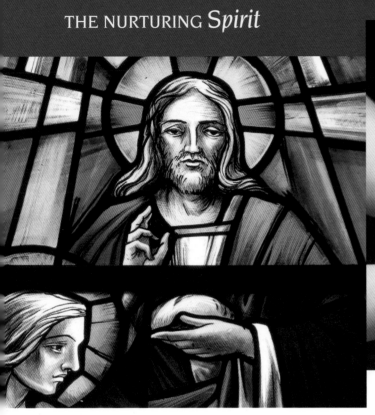

What is the Eucharist?

Christ's own preaching of the Eucharist met with small success. In the synagogue at Capernaum, his claim that he would give his flesh for the life of the world was greeted very unsympathetically. Many of his followers walked away. And, at the Last Supper, with his closest disciples, when he took bread and wine saying, "This is my body... this is my blood poured out for you," one of those with Jesus had the mind to betray him.

To the ancient world the Eucharist seemed "intolerable language" (John 6:60). It appears no more reasonable to the modern world. And so it has been throughout the Church's history. Jesus' claim seems to defy reason. "How can this man give us his flesh to eat?" How can it make sense to suggest that, "Christ becomes present in this sacrament precisely by a change of the bread's whole substance into his body and the wine's whole substance into his blood" (St Thomas Aquinas)?

We must be clear about two things. Firstly, in the Eucharist we are going beyond appearances. In the Eucharist, Christ is as truly present as he was over two thousand years ago in Capernaum. And, even then, people judged only by external appearances: "This is the son of Joseph. We know his father and his mother," they said, "how can he claim to have come down from heaven?... What sign will you give to show us that we should believe in you?" Appearances were deceiving. Appearances *are* deceiving.

Secondly, Christ's presence among men and women was not in itself sufficient to save those who met him. To be saved, they had to approach him in faith. We have to communicate with him. He is present as our food, the eating of which gives us a share in his saving sacrifice and resurrection.

God knows that we human beings are not creatures of spirit only: we are also made of flesh and blood. That's why Jesus became incarnate, took flesh and blood to save us. In the Eucharist Jesus is incarnate again. He comes to us, not only *spiritually* but *physically*, through his presence in the consecrated bread and wine. Like all the sacraments, the Eucharist is more than words, it is a tangible expression of God's love for us. Even in ordinary relationships, a single hug can sometimes mean more than many words. In the Eucharist, Jesus gives us this physical, tangible expression of his self-giving love, to express and sustain our relationship with him.

Sadly, debate about the meaning of the Eucharist has been one of the major points of division between different churches. However, after centuries of argument about how exactly Jesus is present in the Eucharist, there are some encouraging signs of convergence. An important Agreed Statement on the doctrine of the Eucharist has been drawn up by the Anglican-Roman Catholic International Commission, which underlines the importance of this *real, physical and objective presence of Jesus in the sacrament.* The World Council of Churches has also produced a statement of Eucharistic doctrine along similar lines.

To speak of the "objective" presence of Christ in the bread and wine means that it is not limited to the duration of the Eucharist service. In many churches some of the consecrated bread is reserved in a safe called an "aumbry" or "tabernacle", so that it can be taken to sick people who are unable to come to Church. A white or red light always burns near the place where the sacrament is reserved to show that the presence of Christ is focused there in this special way.

"Take, eat; this is my body which is given for you; do this in remembrance of me." In the same way, after supper he took the cup and gave you thanks; he gave it to them saying, "Drink this, all of you; this is my blood of the new covenant, which is shed for you."

Eucharist means thanksgiving

The eating of the bread and wine, which are changed into the Body and Blood of Jesus Christ to be the food of eternal life, is the sign of our union with Christ. In the synagogue in Capernaum Jesus said, "Anyone who does eat my flesh and drink my blood has eternal life, and I shall raise him up on the last day" (John 6:54).

Jesus instituted the Eucharist within the Jewish Passover meal on the night before he died. Jesus said, "I have longed to eat this Passover with you before I suffer; because, I tell you, I shall not eat it again until it is fulfilled in the kingdom of God" (Luke 22:15-16).

Then Jesus took some bread, and when he had given thanks, broke it and gave it to them, saying, "Take, eat; this is my body which is given for you; do this in remembrance of me." In the same way, after supper he took the cup saying, "Drink this, all of you; this is my blood of the new covenant, which is shed for you"(Luke 22:19-20).

In the Eucharist, then, we are united with Christ through the power of the Spirit and so united with the risen Christ's worship of his Father: "... nourished by the body and blood and filled with his Holy Spirit, [we] become one body, one spirit in Christ," and so are able to offer glory and honour to the almighty Father.

The Eucharist unites us with Christ's sacrifice on the cross

On the night before he died, Jesus had instituted the Eucharist to be a sign of his true and continuing presence. To understand the full significance of his presence, then, we look at the full meaning of the sign.

The new Passover meal

According to the first three Gospels, on the night before Jesus died, he celebrated the Passover meal with his disciples, but he changed its meaning, putting himself in the place of the Passover lamb. At the Last Supper Jesus gave us the Eucharist as a new Passover meal, to recall his own sacrifice on the cross, which fulfils all the sacrifices of the old covenant. This is what we re-enact each time we come to the Lord's table.

How does the Eucharist join us with Christ's sacrifice?

When we do this "in remembrance" of what Jesus did on the cross, we are not just looking back at something that happened long ago. Through the Eucharist, his sacrifice becomes present and powerful for us now. Although the cross happened at a point in history, the sacrifice of Christ is timeless, eternal. In the Holy Trinity, the Father, Son and Holy Spirit are in an eternal relationship of self-giving to one another. Through the Eucharist, we are drawn into this eternal relationship of self-giving, sacrificial love. We, for our part, offer our praise, our thanks and all "the work of human hands" symbolised in the bread and wine. But then Christ takes our poor offering, unites it with his perfect offering, and gives us back – himself.

At the Eucharist, in other words, *Christ's* offering becomes *our* offering; for in baptism we became members of Christ's Body. We are not spectators at the sacrifice like the bored soldiers playing dice at Calvary, nor even like Mary and John at the foot of the cross, looking up at the face of the dying Jesus. We are members of Christ's Body. We are united with his sacrifice, "through him, and with him, and in him".

I will not leave you orphans

Jesus had the nicest way of putting things. While preparing his first followers for his departure from this world, he told them, "I will not leave you orphans."

These words of Christ were particularly well-chosen because when we think of orphans we see, in our mind's eye, forlorn and faltering children. And when we think of the apostles we see that, at times, they behaved not like little children but like big children. They argued amongst themselves as to who was the greatest – as to who was the "king of the castle". They made rash promises that they couldn't keep. They got frightened and ran away. Towards the end of his public life they caused an exasperated Jesus to exclaim, "Have I been with you all this time and you still don't understand?" Of course, while he was with them, the apostles didn't understand.

Indeed, they couldn't understand. For while Jesus was with them they could only remain helpless onlookers. Only when Jesus was gone could they begin, literally, to take his place.

Jesus had not only the nicest way of putting things, but also the nicest way of doing things. He promised that through his Spirit he would remain with the apostles and with us. But he would remain in a way that we could easily understand. He would remain through signs or sacraments.

Jesus Christ remains with us through the sign of what came to be known as the "laying on of hands". To the present day, bishops, priests and deacons, in their differing degrees, are ordained or impressed with the priestly character of Christ, by the imposition of hands.

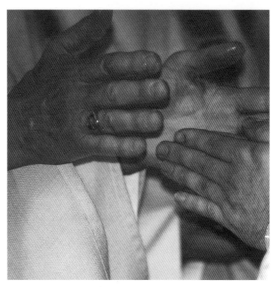

The origin and meaning of the ordained ministry

All baptised Christians share in the royal priesthood of Christ, all are called to offer the sacrifice of thanks and praise, to intercede for others in prayer, to live lives of service and proclaim the Gospel. But the sacrament of holy orders sets men and women apart and empowers them for the service of Christ and the Church in a special way. Ordination is a sacrament because, irrespective of human failing, Christ is made present through the ministry of the ordained individual.

From the first, Jesus set apart special individuals to preach, teach, heal, forgive sins and exercise authority in the Church. He first chose apostles, who were the original founders and ministers of the Church, but as the Church spread and settled down as an institution, and as the first apostles died out, it became necessary to develop a structure whereby the original apostolic authority could be delegated and exercised at the local level. At the earliest stage, as we can read in Acts and the Epistles, leadership was exercised in a number of different ways. But in the second century, partly under the threat to unity from various splinter groups, leadership and authority in the Church became focused in the three ordained ministries: those of bishop, priest and deacon. This has remained so in the "episcopal" churches (Roman Catholic, Orthodox, Anglican and some Lutheran Churches) ever since.

The trusting Spirit
The sacrament of holy orders

Bishops

The bishop is regarded as the direct successor of the apostles, and the fullness of ordained ministry belongs to him or her. (There are now women bishops in some churches of the Anglican Communion.) Within their own area or diocese they are ultimately responsible for all that is done in the name of the Church. In the Anglican Church a new bishop must be ordained (or "consecrated") by at least three other bishops, so that there is a succession of episcopal authority stretching back – in theory at least – to the apostles themselves. The bishop is the focus of unity and authority in each place, a sign of "vertical" unity with the tradition down through history, and of "horizontal" unity with his or her fellow bishops in the worldwide Church. There can therefore be only one diocesan bishop in each diocese, although he or she may be assisted by "suffragan" or "auxiliary" bishops. The ceremonial signs of a bishop are the mitre whose shape symbolises the "tongues of fire" with which the Spirit descended at Pentecost; the crozier or staff, shaped like a shepherd's crook to show that he or she is a chief shepherd; and a ring, which shows that he or she is "wedded" to his or her diocese.

Priests

The English word "priest" is really a shorter form of the Greek word "presbyter", which is usually translated "elder" in the New Testament. For a time, in the early Church, the words "bishop" and "presbyter" seem to have been interchangeable, but as things developed the bishop became the chief pastor, assisted by a number of presbyters who functioned as his deputies. In the modern Church, a priest (as vicar or rector) is normally the focal person in each parish, sometimes assisted by others (curates). The stole (a long "scarf" worn over both shoulders) is a distinctive symbol of the priest's sharing in Christ's priesthood. The priest exercises the apostolic ministry by gathering and moulding the community so that everyone may live and work in the communion of love. He or she does this in the person of Jesus Christ in three principal ways:

■ The priest teaches. The priest's first duty is the proclamation of the Gospel to all. In this way priests fulfil the Lord's command, "Go out to the whole world; proclaim the Good News to all creation." Thus they establish and build up the people of God.

■ The priest makes holy. Having sown the seed of faith through preaching, priests unite their people to God by the administration of the sacraments, especially the celebration of the Eucharist. Through the offering of the Eucharist, the community of believers is established as the Body of Christ.

■ The priest exercises leadership. Having gathered together God's family into the one Body of Christ through the celebration of the sacraments, priests share in the office of Christ, the Leader and Shepherd. Imitating him, priests lead those in their care to a deeper understanding of their own vocation and so build up a genuine Christian community.

Deacons

We read in Acts how "seven men of good reputation" were elected for the daily distribution of alms in order that the apostles could be freed for "prayer and the service of the word". Their number included Stephen, the first Christian martyr, who was stoned to death. Traditionally the appointment of these seven is seen as the origin of the order of deacons. The Greek word "diakonos" which gives us the word "deacon" means "servant". The distinctive mark of a deacon is a stole worn diagonally over one shoulder.

In the early Church, deacons quickly became important as assistants to the bishops. But over the centuries their tasks were divided up and given to others. Today, their early caring role for the sick and poor, and their care of the finances of the community, are usually delegated to lay people in a parish.

Yet the office of a deacon didn't die out altogether. For centuries, in the Western Church, the diaconate was regarded as the last step before the priesthood. St Francis of Assisi remained a deacon all his life. Still today in the Roman Catholic and Anglican churches one must normally spend a year as deacon before being ordained a priest.

However, in both churches there has been a revival of interest in the permanent office of deacon, instead of seeing it merely as a stepping-stone to priesthood. Permanent deacons are chosen from a parish for work with the local priest or bishop. Some have secular jobs, others make it a full-time vocation. With the bishop's permission, deacons may baptise, visit the people, witness marriages, take communion to the sick, conduct funeral services, teach, preach, lead prayer and generally be a leader and animator in the congregation.

What happens at ordination?

■ The ordination usually takes place at the cathedral or some other central church. It always takes place in the context of the Eucharist.

■ Everyone listens to the word of God in scripture.

■ After the sermon, the candidates for the diaconate or priesthood are presented to the bishop, who reminds them of the meaning of their calling.

■ The bishop questions the candidates about their vocation. They promise to accept the authority of holy scripture and the teaching of the Church, to obey those in authority, to be diligent in prayer and study, to try to live according to the Gospel, and to help build up God's people.

■ All pray for the coming of the Holy Spirit to empower the new deacons and priests.

■ The bishop then lays his hands on the head of each candidate and prays, "Send down the Holy Spirit upon your servant (name) for the office and work of a deacon (or priest) in the Church of God."

■ The new deacons or priests are clothed with the appropriate vestments of their order.

■ The bishop hands the newly ordained a copy of the scriptures, as a sign of their authority to preach the Gospel.

■ The bishop may anoint the palms of the priests with the oil of chrism.

■ The sign of peace is exchanged, and the Eucharist continues.

The command to serve

We can plainly read in the Gospels how Christ appointed the apostles to special positions of authority within the new people of God. We should be very careful to notice, however, just what Christ had to say about the way they should use this authority.

> "You know that among the pagans the rulers lord it over them, and their great men make their authority felt. This is not to happen among you. No. Anyone who wants to be great among you must be your servant, and anyone who wants to be first among you must be your slave, just as the Son of Man came not to be served but to serve, and to give his life as a ransom for many" (Matthew 20:25-28).

A few hours before he was crucified, Jesus took a towel and washed the feet of his disciples. There could be no mistaking his intention. The true follower of Christ, no matter what his position amongst the people, must always be the servant of others. And as the apostles set about organising the Church, it was a command they were to keep very much in mind.

The apostles: the foundations of the Church

We have seen that the origins of our faith are rooted in the Jewish people, the people of the Old Testament. This is why Jesus made it perfectly clear in his preaching that he had come not to *destroy* the hopes and desires of the Jewish people but to *fulfil* them. Tragically, only a few were convinced that an augmented people of God had come into existence with the community established by Jesus Christ.

Jesus chooses his apostles

For three years, Jesus travelled around preaching the Good News of the kingdom of God. Gradually, he began to gather around him a small group of followers whom he instructed very carefully. These men and women were to form the nucleus of the new people of God.

It was from among this nucleus that Jesus chose twelve disciples to be the leaders of his Church. These men were to be the foundation members of his new people. They were to be sent out on his business and so he called them "apostles"; in Greek that is exactly what the word means, "those who are sent". After spending a whole night in prayer, Jesus named his apostles: "Simon whom he called Peter, and his brother Andrew, James, John, Philip, Bartholomew, Matthew, Thomas, James, son of Alphaeus, Simon called the Zealot, Judas, son of James, and Judas Iscariot who became a traitor" (Luke 6:14-16).

The choice of the twelve was full of meaning. In the Old Testament the chosen people are often referred to as the twelve tribes of Israel. Jesus was obviously underlining the real link between the new Israel and the old, and stressing at the same time the continuity of God's plan.

Ministries

The word "ministries" comes from the Latin word meaning "to render service". It is used in the Church not simply to describe the ordained ministry but also to describe the different ways in which Christians exercise functions within the Church. These reflect a deepening vision in the Church of the service given by all in the name of the Church.

A ministry has the ultimate aim of preaching and building up the kingdom of God as revealed by Jesus Christ. Each baptised person is called to do this. Different tasks, some officially recognised and others unheralded, are undertaken by individuals to build up the community of believers. They are gifts, St Paul tells us, "to build up the body of Christ until we become one in faith and in the knowledge of God's Son".

How many ministries are there?

Fundamentally there is only one ministry – the ministry of Jesus Christ. It is Jesus Christ who reaches out to serve men and women through the members of his Body, the Church. To help our understanding of this, however, we speak of three different types of ministry:

■ Ministries undertaken by any who are baptised. This refers to any activity which is undertaken without a formal commission from the Church. These ministries would include the work of nurses, teachers and social workers. It is important to recognise that this type of ministry is not limited to the caring professions. It includes the service of all who work in their local parish and do everyday work in a spirit of Christian dedication.

■ The instituted ministries. These are the ministries officially recognised as forms of service within the Church, such as lay readers, youth leaders and teachers, accredited lay workers, musicians, altar servers, wardens and members of the church council.

■ The ordained ministries are those of the diaconate, priesthood and episcopate and are only exercised by those who have received the sacrament of holy orders.

Religious communities

Following Jesus more radically

In the Gospel, Jesus tells a rich young man that if he wants to follow him perfectly he must give away all he has to the poor. In another place he remarks that there are some who "make themselves eunuchs" (i.e. remain celibate and forgo the ties of family life) for the sake of the kingdom of God. And he asks disciples for absolute obedience and commitment as they give up the past, take up their cross and follow him.

From the earliest times, some Christians have found in these commands (sometimes called the "counsels of perfection") a personal challenge and calling to follow Jesus in a more radical way than is possible in ordinary life. This threefold call to poverty, chastity and obedience is the basis of all Christian monastic vows.

The call to solitude

The oldest form of Christian monasticism is the call to lead a solitary life (the word "monasticism" comes from *monos*, meaning "solitary"). St Antony of Egypt, who gave up all his possessions for an extremely austere life of prayer as a hermit, is generally regarded as the founder of monasticism. Many others followed his example, and still today many religious follow the solitary life, especially in the Eastern Orthodox tradition.

Living in community

Most religious, however, live in communities. The oldest and best-known form of community life was founded around the start of the sixth century by St Benedict. Benedict began as a solitary, but having attracted numbers of followers, he formed them into communities whose spiritual and practical life was based on a rule. Essentially the same rule governs the life of communities in the Benedictine order today. It is based around communal worship as the first duty, with private prayer and study, and other forms of work occupying the rest of the time. Some members of the community will be priests, but usually most are lay brothers or sisters.

Different orders

Other forms of communal religious life developed over the centuries. The Cistercian order emerged from a later development of the Benedictine rule, laying greater stress on austerity, silence and solitude.

The Franciscans seek to imitate St Francis' emphasis on poverty and simplicity. They are a mendicant (literally "begging") order, calling themselves "friars" (meaning "brothers") rather than monks, and as well as living partly in community, they also undertake preaching and evangelistic work.

These three are perhaps the best-known, but there are many more religious orders, with varying characters and specialities. Some are enclosed, "contemplative" orders, insisting on their members' seclusion from the world and emphasising the work of adoration and intercession. Others are "active" orders, with members engaged in teaching, medicine or pastoral work. But with differing emphasis, all combine practical and spiritual duties.

At the time of the Reformation in Britain, almost all the religious communities were closed. But they were re-founded in the Anglican Church during the nineteenth century, and by now there are many Anglican Benedictines, Franciscans and other orders around the world.

Tertiaries

Many communities also have "tertiary" or "oblate" members. These are men and women, married or single, who lead ordinary lives in the world, but who attach themselves to a religious community and keep a modified form of vows to suit their state of life. Typically, this involves a fixed rule of prayer and worship, spiritual study, and making a regular retreat with the community.

What's the point?

Sometimes people can't see the purpose of the religious life, or regard it as a waste. Yet the communities perform a very important function. They are reminders of Christ's call to absolute commitment, the striving for perfection. They are havens of peace and prayer in an increasingly noisy, frenzied, prayerless world: places we can go when we need to re-charge our spiritual batteries. Active communities fill a clear practical role of service to the Church and the world. And contemplative ones too, if we believe in prayer, fulfil by their work of intercession a role that is just as vital, and maybe more so. In so many and varied ways, the communities are a precious spiritual asset, a "leaven to the lump" for the whole Church.

The sharing Spirit
The sacrament of marriage

What happens at a wedding?

The priest welcomes everyone present and reminds them of God's purposes in instituting marriage.

The scriptures are read, and a sermon given.

The bride and groom promise to give themselves to one another "for better for worse, for richer for poorer, in sickness and in health, to love and to cherish, till death us do part".

Wedding rings are blessed and exchanged as a sign of the vows that they have taken and a sign that their commitment is unending.

The priest blesses the married couple.

Prayers are offered by everyone present for the couple and their future together.

A celebration of the Eucharist may follow.

The touch of love

There is an old eastern proverb which says, "One look is worth a dozen words and one touch is worth a dozen looks." It's true. Even the lightest touch speaks volumes. It can lift us into another world – the world of love. And it's interesting that many couples who live together end up separating. For even living together in the closest intimacy can leave something lacking in the hunger of the human heart.

A desire to marry is a sign that each partner has been "touched" by another in an extra special way. They have opened their hearts to one another and finally found the courage in their love to want to offer and to receive total commitment for life. There is a risk here for they are offering their whole life to another human being in complete trust. But love, the kind of authentic love which reflects the love of God, does just that; it is willing to give everything, even life itself, for the beloved.

Such a magnificent reflection of God's love is almost too much for us to understand. People often say that they don't understand what a couple see in one another. But love makes it possible for us to see what no one else sees except God: that the one who is loved is uniquely precious, irreplaceable and infinitely loveable. It is natural that those who experience such love want to tell the world and want their love to continue forever.

That is what is at the heart of Christian marriage, that is what is announced to the world on the wedding day. And in that announcement each partner touches the other in a special way; at the heart of the ceremony, the couple take one another's hand and exchange rings as a sign that their love is for life. From that moment on as they touch one another in their love-making, they will re-create their own lives and create a new family as partners with God in the world.

The wedding day completes one period of a relationship and begins another. The love which has been acknowledged and publicly announced now begins to grow and nurture each partner. This takes place in a variety of ways because every marriage is unique. If we look at our hands, the hands that exchange one of the first signs of "touch", we can see how each finger bears its own print – unrepeated on anyone else, ever, at any time.

It's been said that, "like fingerprints, all marriages are different". Each marriage is special, no marriage on earth is quite like another. Regardless of the kind of family a couple come from, their parents' marriage, or the kind of marriage they are "expected" to have, the partners of each marriage have the right and the call from God to create a marriage that is unique to them – based on that unconditional love announced at their wedding.

Sex and love

When we talk about "making love" we usually mean sexual intercourse between two people. But if we stop to think about it "making love" is much more than that. Sexual intercourse can just be a selfish ego trip or simply a desire to follow the crowd. But sexual intercourse is transformed when, in marriage, it becomes a sign of the special love of the couple. This is a love which shows itself in lifelong commitment to one another, in unselfishness, and that, after tension or disagreement, can share genuine forgiveness. This love, expressed in sexual intercourse, is creative in two ways:

■ Each partner re-creates the other: perhaps for the first time, each feels really free and has the trust to share themselves honestly and openly. Each may bring to the marriage scars from earlier relationships or from childhood. Love in marriage helps to heal these hurts. It offers the chance to start again. In the safety of one another's arms each discovers the liberation of true security, new depths, new values. Such experiences transform each partner and help their love to last.

■ New life is created: a special and unique sign of love-making is the creation of a completely new human being. The future of that child will depend very much on the quality of the love in the couple's life together.

God and love

It's so much easier to believe in someone's love for us when we feel their arms about us. The touch of a partner reassures us of their love. It should also reassure us of God's love. For Christians believe that God reaches out and touches us through the love of others. Jesus Christ is at the heart of all love.

Falling in love is a basic human experience. But when we decide to consecrate that love in Christian marriage our human love becomes a sign in the world of God's love. Our experience tells us that there is something "extra" here – something beyond human explanation. When we pledge ourselves to unconditional love for life we show what Christ's own self-sacrificing love is like. Ours, like his, is a love without limits. We are in true partnership with God.

It's not surprising, then, that we are offered God's own supreme love to strengthen and sustain us and to make perfect love possible. That is what is at the heart of Christian marriage. This mystery and miracle of love, the sacrament of marriage, is indeed a partnership with God. God is involved, intimately, in the relationship.

Faithfulness matters

Following the words of Jesus himself, the Church teaches very strongly that marriage is for life. The reasons for this are both practical and spiritual. The practical reason is that we all need security in love and our personal life, and love that only depends on physical attraction and sexual passion is scarcely worth the name. Children, particularly, need a secure home, and risk being badly damaged by their parents splitting up. The spiritual reason is that by learning to love faithfully and unselfishly across good times and bad, we are actually learning to love as God loves, growing in God's image, and preparing to share God's life in heaven. Both reasons make it crucial that couples receive all possible support and try to make the marriage work even in times of difficulty. It is the most common experience of couples that sticking together through the bad times usually brings them through to a deeper commitment and a stronger love.

Unmarried people

Sometimes the Church seems to emphasise marriage and the family so much that others feel left out. The Church is for everyone – and many people, perhaps most nowadays, do not fit the conventional family pattern. What does the Church say to them – remembering that all of us have sexual feelings and instincts?

Celibate people are those who feel positively that their vocation and fulfilment lie in the single life, and the Church has always honoured this choice. St Paul says that the single person may have more time and energy than others to serve the Lord (1 Corinthians 7:32-35). Many feel called and able to redirect their instincts of sexual love into other kinds of relationships which are loving and fulfilling but not sexually expressed. The Church and society have been served well by countless celibate lay people, as well as by celibate clergy, and by religious brothers and sisters who lead the celibate life in community.

But not all people who are single feel it as a positive vocation. Some would dearly wish to find a partner. Others have been widowed, or suffered the break-up of relationships. Some are single parents, who might hope to find a permanent partner. All have their place of welcome in Christ's Church as they seek to find and fulfil God's call in their personal life.

People having same-sex attraction have been treated with little understanding in the past, and often with cruelty and rejection. Happily this has begun to change. In a recent statement, the bishops of the Church of England call on churches to offer welcome and support. They also call on people with a homosexual orientation who conscientiously do not believe they are called to celibacy to reject promiscuity and build faithful, lasting relationships. This insistence on faithfulness is not to force people with a homosexual orientation to "copy" heterosexual marriage, but is based on the conviction that we are all made in God's image. Sex is meant to express and sustain a covenant of faithful love – in other words, the same kind of love that God shows us.

Divorce and re-marriage

Nevertheless the Church recognises that some marriages, sadly, will reach a point of irretrievable breakdown. Those who go through this experience need the Church's fullest measure of love, support and welcome, and the comfort of word, worship and sacrament. The Church also welcomes those who, after the failure of a previous marriage, have married again. Because of the nature of the wedding vows – which are made "till death us do part" – second marriages do not usually take place in church, but are blessed after a civil ceremony. Sometimes this causes hurt, but most Christians feel that in a society where divorce is becoming increasingly common, it is important for us to uphold the teaching that marriage should be for life. At the same time, Jesus warned us against judging others – all of us fall short of the ideal, and fail to love as we ought.

The wedding ring

Rings have always been rich in symbolism. In Biblical times they were made of ivory, crystal or metal and were a sign of dignity and rank. Increasingly, they signified a pledge of loyalty and trust and, in Roman times, were used as a mark of betrothal.

Since the Middle Ages, it has been traditional for the bridegroom to place the ring on the thumb of the bride, then on her second finger, and then on her third, naming each person in the Trinity. The ring was then placed on the fourth finger at the word "Amen". This shows in action as well as in words that he enters marriage "in the name of the Father and of the Son and of the Holy Spirit".

Another reason in ancient times for placing the ring on the fourth finger is because it was believed that it contained a certain vein directly linked to the heart.

The ring is not a symbol of captivity; rather of unbroken unity and unending changelessness – the perfect round. It does not mean that "this person belongs to me" but "I belong to this person".

Rings at a wedding are blessed with these or similar words: *Heavenly Father, by your blessing, let these rings be to those who wear them a symbol of unending love and faithfulness, to remind them of the vow and covenant they have made this day; through Jesus Christ our Lord. Amen.*

To understand our humanity, what it is to be human, we need to look at Jesus Christ. Jesus was truly God; he was the Son who lived amongst us as a fully human person. He was exactly the same as us in all things. He ate like us, he laughed and cried like us, he loved like us and his body was vulnerable and could suffer and be destroyed as ours can. The only difference between Jesus' humanity and ours was that sin played no part in his life. He did not sin. And the reason he did not sin was because he was truly human. He was fully human exactly as God had intended every man and woman to be. He is a pattern for humanity. Jesus shows us what it is to be a true and complete human being.

The healing Spirit
The sacrament of reconciliation

Sin enters our life when we are less than human. Every time we think, say or do something which is not a reflection of Jesus' humanity, we are less than human; we sin. But sin doesn't stop there, because so much of what we do or fail to do affects other people. The knock-on effect of damaging relationships, isolation, breakdowns in communication, all serve to cut us off from others, and so distort and damage people. We even say in extreme cases, "He/she's like an animal!" What we're saying when we say that is in a sense true – that person is less than fully human, but then so are those who caused that distortion or damage, that isolation. It's easy to see that sin damages not only individuals but also whole communities.

Throughout his life Jesus worked and preached endlessly amongst all sorts of people to bring down the barriers which divided them. He emphasised over and over again that we are all God's children, we are God's family, God's chosen people. Following his resurrection, Jesus' followers gathered together and became a community. They were united in that they were listening to the words of Jesus and experiencing his active love in the work of his Spirit in their lives. They knew what it was to be fully human but they were also still very weak and easily discouraged.

Even in the first accounts of the early Church, we can read about tensions, disagreements and rejection within this community of believers. Clearly, in spite of all that they had experienced, they remained fragile and many of them carried within them the damage caused by sin (by being less than human) from past years.

No one becomes fully human overnight or even in a year or two. It takes time. And while we are growing towards full humanity we need to experience the healing, reconciling action of the Holy Spirit. The Church celebrates that action in the sacrament of reconciliation.

Through this sacrament we are renewed and recommitted to being open to the action of the Spirit in our lives in helping us to become more fully human and so be effective in reflecting Christ and his words of life and love to others. In this way we strengthen Christ's Body on earth, his community, which in turn can continue the healing, saving, loving work of Jesus Christ.

The healing truth

One of the great values of confession is that, for once, it makes us stop pretending and allows us to tell the truth about ourselves. Isn't it true that for much of the time we are playing an act? We cover up what's really going on in our hearts and minds and live behind a mask. Sometimes we do it for the best of reasons, sometimes the reasons are not so good. Even those who know us and love us best might be appalled to know what lurks in the dustier corners of our personal lives, and it appalls us too sometimes, which is why we are very careful about which bits of ourselves we reveal

to different people. But, of course, God knows the *real* us: it's the *real* us he has to deal with, and it's the *real* us he loves.

Confession cuts through all the garbage of illusion with which we try to fool others – and ourselves – and it makes us examine and pronounce to someone else what we are really like. For obvious reasons, that can be difficult and there's no denying that it takes some guts. But at the same time it can turn into a wonderful experience, because, in the end, you realise there wasn't anything to be afraid of. Because, absolution means that we really are forgiven; it means God really does love and accept you: not just the Sunday-best you, but the *real* you. And it can be such a relief not to have to pretend any more.

Healing, holiness and wholeness

Confession is about holiness and wholeness. Holiness and wholeness are very closely connected. A lot of people think that to be holy you have to suppress all the sinful, difficult bits of yourself and pretend they're not there. But in fact the opposite is true. Real holiness – wholeness – means developing all the bits of you, but in their proper function – and that includes all the mean, nasty, unacceptable bits we try to hide but that will keep popping up to worry us. God made everything we are, and God's purpose isn't to reduce or destroy parts of us but to restore and recreate us to be more fully and more richly ourselves. Evil never created anything. All it can do is spoil aspects of us that God made good. And God is going to reclaim every part of us. God wills that not one hair of our head should be lost. But, first, what is wrong in us has to be opened up to God by our own act of will, so that God can heal it and love it back to its original purpose. That's the only way we can ever become the glorious people God made us to be.

Can't we confess our sins on our own?

Yes, of course, and, when it's done and meant, God is certainly present and ready to forgive. Yet it's often only in the presence of another person that the reality of one's self and one's sin strikes home. God knows we are not too good at realising spiritual things in a purely internal way. As with all the sacraments, it is the *objectivity* of sacramental confession that makes it such a strength. You are absolved in God's name, and you go away knowing, absolutely, that you are absolved. Recently, a family doctor wrote that over half his patients were not so much physically ill as troubled psychologically or emotionally or socially. And he mentioned how much he wished he could give some sort of official absolution to so many of them loaded down with an intolerable sense of guilt or rejection or depression. Simply to be able to say, "Look: this burden has been taken away. You are accepted, you are wanted, you are loved. Now go and live..."

Why confess to a priest?

The short answer is that that's what priests are for. In the *Book of Common Prayer*, when a bishop ordains a priest he lays his hands on his or her head and says to him, "Whose sins you forgive they are forgiven; whose sins you retain they are retained." Those words were first spoken by Jesus to the apostles on the day of the resurrection, and ever since then that authority to pronounce forgiveness has been handed down in the ordained ministry of the Church. Some people find that hard to accept because it seems to put the priest in a superior role as some kind of judge. But that's really not the idea. The priest is a sinner just as much as the penitent. It's important that the very last words the priest says in confession are, "Please pray for me, a sinner also"; and he or she means it, because there is in fact nothing quite as humbling as the privilege of helping another soul to be open to God. The priest is just another human sinner whom Christ happens to have given this job of embodying and declaring his forgiveness – Christ's forgiveness, not the priest's – to those who ask for it. It is also important to know that there are no circumstances under which a priest may divulge what is said in the confessional.

The importance of sincerity

Like all the sacraments, confession can be abused. You can confess mechanically and carelessly, just as you can come to communion mechanically and carelessly. There has to be real sincerity, real facing up, real sorrow for sin, and a real resolve to do better. But, though the sacrament can be abused, other people's *ab*use of it doesn't argue for my *dis*use of it – any more than in the case of communion. Of course it isn't always easy, and we shouldn't pretend otherwise. It is deeply personal, because it is meant to be, and sometimes it involves saying embarrassing things. But perhaps the more we are embarrassed by the thought of it, the more we are in need of it.

When should we go to confession?

It depends on you. There is no rule. Many Anglicans have a regular appointment to see their confessor, say every two or three months. Often their confession will be combined with spiritual direction – a general discussion of their spiritual state and growth. Others go when they feel the need, or when something particular is troubling their conscience. You can, of course, choose to talk to any priest. You can also decide the way you conduct confession: whether in the more traditional way, at a kneeling desk beside the priest, or simply sitting and talking together. If you are shy of making an appointment and prefer to confess "anonymously", there are churches which advertise confessions at regular times, and you simply turn up and wait your turn at the confessional.

What happens at confession?

☐ In thought and prayer the penitent prepares beforehand what to talk about in confession.

☐ The penitent and priest meet together. The penitent may kneel or sit, depending on the circumstances. Usually the penitent is given a printed card with an opening and closing form of words.

☐ The priest blesses the penitent with a prayer that he or she will be strengthened to make a good confession.

☐ The penitent reads the opening words, "I confess to Almighty God, to the whole company of heaven, and before you, that I have sinned…" The penitent then continues in his or her own words, then closes with the prayer on the card.

☐ The priest tries to give helpful advice about what has been said, with words of encouragement and a reminder of Christ's healing, welcoming love.

☐ The priest suggests a prayer, psalm or some other text to be said later by the penitent as an act of thanksgiving (this is sometimes misnamed a "penance", but it mustn't be thought of as a punishment).

☐ The priest pronounces the Prayer of Absolution, declaring God's forgiveness.

☐ The priest blesses the penitent and says, "Please pray for me, a sinner also."

"Christ has given power and commandment to his Church to pardon the offences of all who truly repent and turn to him; and by his authority committed to me, I absolve you in the name of the Father and of the Son and of the Holy Spirit."

The saving Spirit
The anointing of the sick

When we are sick we feel alone, weak and frightened. Things which seemed important don't matter much anymore. But, as Christians, we know that we are never alone. In fact, we are never so close to Jesus as when we are weak or unwell.

During his life on earth, Jesus loved people into total health. He lifted up those who were sick and raised them to new life.

When the time was right, Jesus accepted pain and death. And then, on the cross, Jesus transformed suffering. Through suffering he was raised to new life. And Jesus offers the same life to all who accept him in faith.

Throughout our lives, Jesus loves us into total health, helping us to triumph over our sickness. For, at the heart of being a Christian, are the healing sacraments in which Jesus comes to us as a constant source of strength and restoration.

■ In baptism, we join the family of God and celebrate God's love and care for us.

■ In reconciliation, we experience the healing power of Jesus Christ and the peace of mind which only he can give.

■ In the Eucharist, we are strengthened and supported by the true presence of Jesus every time we turn to him.

The anointing of the sick is the ultimate healing sacrament, available whenever our health is seriously impaired by sickness or old age. God is always with us in our illness, loving us into health of mind, body and soul. Through our faith we know that we will have life for ever.

Throughout his life, Jesus loved people so deeply and so completely that they were healed of whatever was destroying them, whether that was physical or mental illness, or emotional or spiritual suffering. That is what he continues to do when we receive the sacrament of the sick.

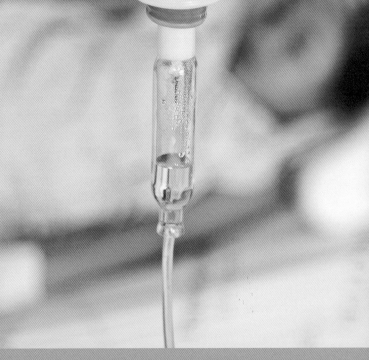

Our fears for the future begin to dissolve as we listen to the words of Jesus who promises to be with us for ever.

Through this sacrament, the sick person is strengthened and encouraged as he or she face any anxiety or fear he or she may have about frailty or death. Faith is renewed and the tendency in illness to despair and hopelessness is overcome by the loving signs of the Lord's presence at this special time in his or her life.

Old age

The frailty of old age is recognised too. An older person may not be ill, but the years do impose burdens upon the elderly that can be difficult to adjust to and that can make the older person feel isolated and, at times, very lonely. Again, this sacrament helps and strengthens Christians in this stage of life so that they can continue to be part of the family of God as actively as possible, for older people have so much to offer younger Christians.

Children

A sick child has special difficulties to overcome. The normal activity and liveliness of youth are often limited to a considerable extent through illness. Being confined to bed or to the house for long periods can limit social contact with other children and a sick child can often worry about the stress their illness places upon parents and the rest of the family. The sacrament of the sick is for any sick child who is old enough to understand what it means and how it can help them as a sign of the real involvement of Jesus Christ in their life day by day.

A sign of life

Some people have the idea that this sacrament signifies approaching death – it is only offered when all hope is lost. In fact the reverse is true: it is a sign of life, the eternal life promised by Jesus Christ, here and now as well as in the future. Christ came to show us how we can have life to the full in whatever situation we find ourselves. His Spirit, active and dynamic in our sickness and frailty as well as in our health and strength, is a real presence. The sacrament of the sick confirms this in a tangible way.

One of the prayers used for blessing the sick person following reception of the sacrament of the sick is:

The almighty Lord, who is a strong tower for all who put their trust in him, whom all things in heaven, on earth, and under the earth obey, be now and evermore your defence. May you believe and trust that the only name under heaven given for health and salvation is the name of our Lord Jesus Christ.

God is with the sick person now, nothing is more certain than that. In our growing closeness to Christ through faith celebrated in this sacrament we receive a new vision of life, a vision that sees everything in the light of God's eternal love. This love is lasting; no sickness is final and even death cannot withstand such love. When we are anointed with oil, a symbol of healing in Christ's time, we receive a sign of Christ's healing care for us now. Only his strength can lift us out of suffering to joy and peace.

"Any one of you who is ill should send for the elders of the church, and they must anoint the sick person with oil in the name of the Lord and pray over him. The prayer of faith will save the sick person and the Lord will raise him up again; and if he has committed any sins, he will be forgiven."

James 5:14-15

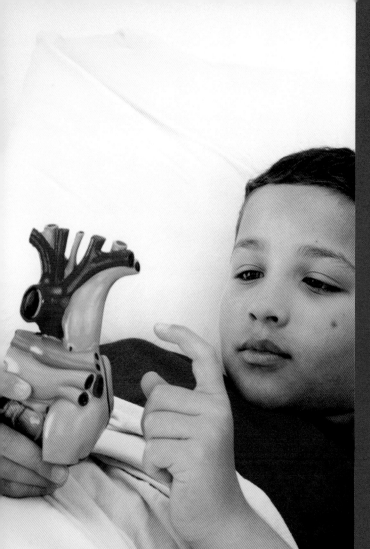

What happens at the anointing of the sick?

This sacrament may be celebrated at the church either during a celebration of the Eucharist or at a service for those who are sick. More frequently, it is celebrated at home, during a house communion, or in a hospital or nursing home.

■ The family, friends and Christian community gather together with the priest.

■ In preparation for the sacrament, all who are present call to mind their personal failure to live as Christians. Prayers of sorrow and reconciliation are expressed.

■ Everyone listens to the word of God read from the scriptures.

■ Prayers are offered for all who are sick and for the person receiving the sacrament.

■ Following Christ's example, the priest lays his hands on the sick person in silence.

■ The sick person is then anointed on the forehead and the hands as the priest prays for them.

■ Everyone present prays the Lord's Prayer and Holy Communion may now be distributed. This is followed by a final prayer of blessing and healing.

The laying on of hands

After speech and facial expressions, the most powerful vehicle of human communication must surely be the hands. Dictators use sawing, sweeping gestures to the tumultuous roars of a hysterical crowd. The hands of a conductor chart rhythmic movements as the orchestra is guided at one moment into soft and peaceful melodies, at another into passionate fortissimmi. When the police officer raises his or her hand the traffic comes to a halt. A wave says, "goodbye" or, "welcome home". A caressing hand says, "You are beautiful." An embrace says, "I love you."

The liturgy of the Church is full of bodily gestures that are rich in meaning but which may easily escape our notice. The laying on of hands in the sacrament of the sick is such a gesture. When, after the introduction, the priest places his hands on the sick person's head for a few moments, no words are spoken. There is complete silence. What does that mean? The gesture itself is borrowed from Jewish tradition and it has many meanings. It is a sign of blessing, as when Jacob blessed the sons of Joseph (Genesis 48:14). It is also a sign that the Spirit of God is coming to consecrate someone for a special task, for example, priests (Numbers 8:10). Another meaning is that it is a symbol of union: when a sacrifice was to be offered, those making the offering would lay their hands on the victim as if to say, "I am one with you; you are to take on my sentiments of thanksgiving

or sorrow or adoration, and so, I will be united with you when you are offered in sacrifice" (see, for example, Leviticus 1:4).

Some of these meanings are still preserved in the other sacraments like baptism, reconciliation, confirmation and ordination. In the sacrament of the sick, the laying on of hands has a special meaning. First of all, it signifies blessing and healing. Jesus blessed the children in this way, he cured the woman afflicted with a painful stoop and restored sight to the blind man at Bethsaida. He promised that his "disciples will lay hands on the sick and they will be healed" (Mark 16:18). Straight away we see this practice in the early Church. After St Paul has become blind, Ananias comes and lays his hands on him and his sight is restored (Acts 9:17-19).

So when the priest lays hands on the sick person's head, he or she is following the instructions of Jesus and the practice of the apostles. They are praying, not with words but with a gesture, for healing. The healing, of course, will not be brought about just by a gesture or even by the priest. The gesture or action is what we see. What we don't see is the internal, hidden thing that is happening. The Spirit of God is released in the sick person who is disposed to receive the Spirit. The Spirit of God comes with healing and peace for the body, mind and soul. For the Spirit, after all, was called "the Comforter" by Jesus.

Our final communion in this life, which we may receive when we are seriously ill or dying, has been traditionally called by its Latin name "Viaticum", which means "the way". It is the sacrament of the way... to eternal life, to our heavenly Father, in perfect peace.

Our first invitation to become a member of God's family was accepted at our baptism and confirmed by us at our confirmation. We have had the life of Christ within us strengthened continually through Holy Communion and many of us have received special help in living our vocations in marriage or holy orders. When we have turned away from God, grown weak, careless and unloving, we have been continually welcomed back to our heavenly Father's family through the sacrament of reconciliation. In old age or sickness we have been healed from any spiritual ill and, sometimes, healed physically too if this would be of benefit to us spiritually, by the anointing of the sick.

Reborn in the Spirit
The death of a Christian

A t the end of our life it is time to go home. God has kept God's promise to us all of our life. God will always remain faithful. There is a great consolation in our faith for anyone who has suffered the sadness and pain which accompanies the death of someone we love. For the faithful, life is changed, not ended, and the bond of union in the Body of Christ unites us still.

We can see that death, to some extent, is natural, since everything that lives on this earth dies, if only to allow new life to spring up. That does not take away its pain. God did not make men and women to die. In fact, at first sight, the philosopher who said that death is absurd would seem to be right.

Life is of God

But then we read St Paul, and we learn that death came into this world because of sin. That explains it. The only real life is of God. And God's creatures are privileged to share it. When any creature tries to make itself independent of God, then it loses life. To be without God is to be dead. The wages of sin is death.

Death became the hallmark on human nature once human beings sinned. The Son of God became human so he took on the hallmark of human nature. He died because of sin. Now, this is the miracle: he took our nature willingly, lovingly and

accepted death as its price. And his love was such that death could not triumph over it. Christ's death defeated death itself. That is what makes the cross of Christ the sign of victory over sin, because it was victorious over death.

Christ took men and women back to his Father. This meant he showed his love for his Father by giving his life totally. His death, then, was the way to the Father, a stepping stone to the Father. Death could no longer have the last word; it had lost its sting. Death had become the gateway to the life of the resurrection. That does not take away the pain of the cross but it gives it purpose. Love is shown in pain, and he who loves greatly suffers much.

The Christian is not better than Jesus Christ, nor has any other way to the Father been found but by the same way of the cross. For some it is a light burden, for others heavy, but it is for everyone. Everyone must die, but we do it by stages. It is St Paul who tells us that we have died already in baptism. It is clear what he means: we have died to sin. We must have, because we have begun to share in the new life of Christ risen from the dead.

That is what being a Christian means – sharing his life, literally. If we have risen, we must have died. Yes, we have died to sin, but not finally, unfortunately, and that is the root of the problem. We can still sin, until the day we finally die. But every day, in trying to die a little more to sin, the Christian lives more deeply in Christ.

If we make a success of that, dying in the end won't be a problem. It will simply be the confirmation of our whole life's purpose. Death will not break our union with Christ but establish it for ever.

Judgement

"Judgement" sometimes conveys images of a balancing act on the heavenly scales of justice; with the good actions of our lifetime on the one side and the bad ones on the other. Or we think of the judgement as a trial in which God sums up, while we listen in agonised suspense, and then God passes a decision which could have us dragged away screaming for mercy or protesting our innocence. But judgement is not like that at all.

The truth is that we will be our own judge. We save or condemn ourselves according to the way we judge Christ. Such is the power of Christ's words that our salvation or condemnation depends on our reaction to them. If we believe in Christ's words *and accept them* they will fill us with eternal life. But if we reject his words they will destroy us.

Go into a room on a summer evening when the sun is streaming through the window. The rays of the sun light up the room in a way that no artificial light can; everything seems transformed. But within those rays of light every little speck of dust and every little mark shows up with amazing clarity. The air about us is full of activity and hidden elements. Only by drawing a curtain and keeping out the bright sunlight can we eliminate such an exposure by the light.

The words of Christ have the power of light. They show us what is in a man or woman, but some cannot accept it. They try to "draw a curtain" to shut out the light that is Christ.

"You want to kill me," says Jesus, "because nothing I say has penetrated into you" (John 8:37).

It is a sad truth that, so often, we resent the goodness in other people. Their virtue shows up our own faults and failings and so we try to bring them down to size – our size. We behave, indeed, as Christ's accusers did. We judge. And by our judgement we are condemned with our own lips.

It would be wrong, therefore, to fear judgement as we fear the unknown. Judgement – and heaven or hell which follows – is known to us only too well. If our present life is one of hatred, of vengeance, walled up from the care of others, we are already experiencing something of the agony of hell. Our rejection of God and goodness, because we prefer selfishness and sin, can only lead to a continuation of the world we have built up for ourselves – in eternity. Men and women are not cast into hell; they themselves create it.

On the other hand, if our present life is one of trying to receive Christ's words by accepting his brothers and sisters, even to the extent of "giving a cup of cold water in his name", we need have no fear of what follows judgement. Christ's words of welcome will show us up for what we are, "Come, you whom my Father has blessed, take for your heritage the kingdom prepared for you since the foundation of the world" (Matthew 25:34).

Why should we pray for the dead?

There is a well-established tradition in the Church of praying for the dead, but why should it be considered necessary? Isn't the purpose of life on earth seen as a preparation for life after death – becoming fit for heaven, for eternal life?

Of course, we hope and trust that in our Christian life on earth we are gradually learning what it means to love God and other people, and so becoming fit for life in perfect union with God, which is what heaven is. But we know from experience that life often leaves a person spiritually incomplete. Few of us could claim to be sure that when we die we shall be so united with God and our fellow human beings that we shall be fit for the divine life. That is why the mainstream of Christian thinking has held to the view that there must be an intermediate state between death and our final, complete union with God in heaven.

Traditionally, this state has been called "Purgatory", but it is not a very helpful word. We are not meant to think of it as a state of punishment but of growth in the love of God, a continuation of earthly life where all that is good in us will be perfected and all that is wrong will be healed.

We can pray for the departed because Jesus has assured us that we are one Body with all his people, living and departed, and so, all the members of the Body should care and pray for one another, whether we happen to be this side of the grave or beyond it. In Jesus, death and time do not separate us. So, just as we pray for one another as we live and grow on earth, it is natural and right to pray for those who have passed on to the next stage of their spiritual journey. In the same way, we can be sure that the departed in Christ and all the saints made perfect in heaven continue to pray and care for us.

New life

Death is a rebirth. Our first birth is that moment when, as a baby, we break out from the womb into a new world. As a baby within the security of the womb we cannot contemplate what the world outside is like. Birth is a shocking experience yet it is necessary for life and for growth beyond imagination. In our present world, the womb in which we now live, we cannot speak intelligently of what awaits us. The scriptures speak of death as a new birth when we break out of the womb and enter a new creation. The next world into which we are born is the kingdom of God beyond our imagining.

"I think that what we suffer in this life can never be compared to the glory, as yet unrevealed, which is waiting for us... From the beginning till now the entire creation, as we know, has been groaning in one great act of giving birth; and not only creation, but all of us who possess the first-fruits of the Spirit, we too groan inwardly as we wait for our bodies to be set free" (Romans 8:18-23).

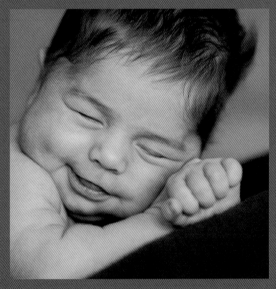

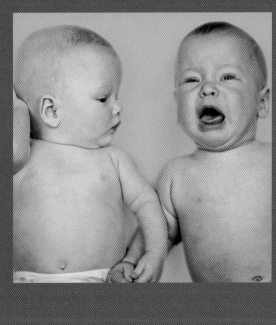

The communion of saints

A saint, from the Latin *sanctus* meaning "holy", is one who shares in the divine life of Christ. The New Testament refers to the "poor saints in Jerusalem" and in *Acts*, St Luke refers to Peter visiting the "saints in Lydda", one of whom he cured from paralysis (Acts 9:32).

Saints are the sort of people who are never satisfied with a "doing what we've always done" approach to life. There is never the slightest chance of them falling into a rut, because saints are men and women who want to do what Jesus wants. And that can lead to a very exciting life. "They are led," wrote Fr John Dalrymple, "into mad escapades of folly and scandal like Franz Jägerstätter refusing to serve in the German Army when everyone else did, or like Charles de Foucauld, going off to live with the Saharan Tuareg as one of them."

Now, this tendency to approach life in completely novel and fresh ways makes it very difficult to say exactly what a saint is. There is no ready-made mould into which we can pour the required virtues needed to make a saint.

We sometimes think we have the gift of recognising true sanctity, but if it were possible to choose any saint from the Church's calendar and invite him or her to dinner, we would probably get quite a shock. Plaster statues of very calm and quiet-looking saints serve to remind us that the saints are always ready to help and keep their memory before us. But they rarely capture the energy and enthusiasm of men and women who are always ready to turn the world on its head.

The truth, of course, is that many biographies of the saints down the years have made them out to be solemn-faced fanatics. Good fanatics, holy fanatics, but fanatics none the less. And that's a great pity, for it has left us with a stereotype image of the saint that not many of us fancy imitating. After all, who wants to be a fanatic?

To understand the true greatness of the saint, we have always to remember that saints are men and women of flesh and blood. The canonised saints were people with limitations just like the rest of us. They were people who allowed God's grace to work in them and, even after they had attained great holiness, kept their own distinctive personalities. First and foremost, a saint is a human being. What makes the saint different from the rest of us is a complete openness to the promptings of the Spirit.

There is a saint and a sinner in all of us. But if we do choose to be a saint, to follow the promptings of the Spirit, we will be an entirely unique kind of saint. For as Evelyn Waugh once wrote, "There is only one saint that Bridget Hogan can actually become, St Bridget Hogan. She cannot slip into heaven in fancy dress, made up as St Joan of Arc."

"*The Holy Spirit will come upon you*"

Mary

Why all the fuss about Mary?

A lot of people are frightened of making a fuss of Mary because they think it detracts from the worship of God. Certainly, it is wrong to confuse devotion to Mary with the worship that is due to God alone. The point about Mary is that she was an ordinary girl, a peasant from the poorest part of Palestine. But – and it's a very big but – she was an ordinary girl chosen to do the most extraordinary thing, to become the Mother of God the Son.

This poem by Mary Coleridge says about Mary, bluntly but truly:

> Mother of God! No lady thou,
> But common woman of common earth.
> "Our Lady" ladies call thee now,
> But Christ was never of gentle birth:
> A common man of the common earth.
> Never a lady did God choose,
> But only a maid of low degree,
> So humble she might not refuse
> The carpenter of Galilee –
> A daughter of the people she.

If we get too sugary about Mary we'll forget why she really is important. Most of what we hear about her comes from Luke's Gospel, and Luke is very clear that Mary represents the humble people of Israel, the underclass, the losers and victims. The words which Mary says in Luke's Gospel are nearly all quotations from Old Testament passages about the poor. Mary is their voice, the voice of the voiceless, which God at last has heard.

Think about the song that Mary sings when the angel tells her she is to give birth to the Saviour. That song, called the "Magnificat", is said and sung over and over again in

cathedrals and churches, and people hardly ever stop to think how revolutionary the words are. "God will scatter the proud and arrogant in their conceit", Mary sings. "He will put down the mighty from their thrones, and exalt the humble and meek. He will fill the starving with good things and send the rich away empty" (Luke 1:46-55). Mary is the symbol of God's care for the poor, and God's promise of justice.

Mary and the humble, suffering people of God

Mary doesn't only represent the economically poor and struggling: she represents the socially rejected as well. As far as the world was concerned, Mary was an unmarried mother and Jesus illegitimate. It's still hard enough to be illegitimate or an unmarried mother these days, but in first-century Palestine it was a great deal worse. Yet despite the pain it would bring her, Mary submitted to God's will and answered God's call with an unwavering "Yes".

So even from the first, Jesus and Mary were marked by a struggle that they had to bear together; and that's only part of the suffering that she had to share with him. When Mary took Jesus to the temple, the old man Simeon prophesied that Jesus would be the light of the Gentiles, but then Simeon turned to Mary and said, "Behold, a sword shall pierce through your heart too" (Luke 2:35). From time to time in the Gospels we see glimpses of Mary following Jesus, trying to understand, "storing these things up in her heart" until the day when it did become clear. Eventually Simeon's prophecy was fulfiled on Good Friday, when the Gospel says she and St John stood at the foot of the cross when all the rest of them had run away. And in his last words Jesus said to John, the beloved disciple, "Behold thy mother", and to Mary, "Behold thy Son" (John 19:25-27).

Mary, Mother of God

The title "Mother of God", which is given to Mary, can cause some confusion. There is only one way to become a member of the human race and that is to be born of a woman. God who created us wanted to be right at the heart of creation and so wanted to become human too. God became human in the person of Jesus Christ, and Mary was his mother.

In Jesus Christ, God became human. Jesus Christ is truly God and truly human. He is the one mediator between God and ourselves. He brings heaven to earth and men and women to God. Mary, as the human mother of Jesus Christ, can be called the "God-bearer".

During the first five centuries of the Church, there were many theories going around about how Jesus Christ was both God and human. Some emphasised his divinity, others were more concerned with his humanity. Finally, the Council of Ephesus in AD 431 resolved the argument by declaring Jesus Christ as being truly God and truly human. Consequently, the Council also stated that Mary was not only the Mother of Christ, but also the Mother of God. If we say that Mary is not the Mother of God then Jesus Christ is not God and we are not saved. The title is, in fact, saying more about Jesus Christ than about Mary.

Mary, then, is truly the Mother of God if two conditions are fulfilled: that she is really the mother of Jesus and that Jesus is really God.

Finally, having stood by him to the end, Mary shared in the joy of the resurrection, and the final glimpse we get of Mary in scripture is at Pentecost, where she receives the Holy Spirit along with the twelve disciples (Acts 1:14, 2:1-4).

Devotion to Mary in the Church

It is because of her unique closeness to Jesus that we remember her so often in church with special feasts and prayers, pictures and statues. As we have seen, the important thing about Mary and about all the saints is that they are not just historical figures, they are alive and with us now. When we stand up and say in the Creed, "We believe in the communion of saints", we are declaring that we are united in fellowship with all Christ's people, whether they happen to be this side of the grave or beyond it. The reason we have pictures and statues in church is to help remind us that they are there, even though we can't see them.

It's no different from having photographs of our ordinary friends and loved ones to remember them by. The saints are our friends too: we have "friends on earth and friends above", as the hymn says. After the Lord's Prayer, the best known prayer in Christendom is the Hail Mary. It is composed of the words of the angel Gabriel and Elizabeth, spoken to Mary in Luke's Gospel, followed by the request that she will pray for us.

Hail Mary, full of grace, the Lord is with thee; blessed art thou among women, and blessed is the fruit of thy womb, Jesus. Holy Mary, Mother of God, pray for us sinners now and at the hour of our death.

Mary is bound to be special among saints, because who else could be closer to Christ than the one who gave him flesh, who carried him, suckled, washed, fed, clothed, taught him, and who finally held him dead in her arms? The Gospel itself makes it clear that we should honour her. When Elizabeth says, "Of all women you are the most blessed. Why should I be so honoured, that the mother of the Lord should come to me?", she is really speaking on behalf of us all (Luke 1:42-43). And when on the cross, Jesus gave Mary to be the mother of the beloved disciple, the Church has always taken that to mean that he was giving her to be the mother of all his beloved disciples, mother of Christians and mother of the Church. The Church is a family after all, and what's a family without a mother?

That's why we say the Hail Mary and honour her and ask her to pray for us: because she is not some sort of goddess, but on the contrary, someone who was regarded as the lowest of the low, but who obeyed God's will, carried his Son into the world, who shared in his suffering more closely than anyone else, and who therefore now shares in his glory. That's why, as Gabriel foretold, all generations have called her blessed, and always will.

> Now you too, in him, have heard the message of the truth and the good news of your salvation, and have believed it; and you too have been stamped with the seal of the Holy Spirit of the Promise, the pledge of our inheritance which brings freedom for those whom God has taken for his own, to make his glory praised.
>
> **Ephesians 1:13-14**